Kidnapped

The true story of my captivity in Iran

Linda Davies

First published in the US, 2014, by Vigliano Books

ISBN: 9798675030088

Praise for Linda Davies and *Kidnapped*

'No thriller can be as thrilling as the true story told by Davies.' ***Ed Epstein, investigative journalist and author***

'An example of how dangerous even idyllic parts of the world can be… The waiting and fear of the unknown; how hard it is to keep up morale; and how innocent acts can turn dangerous. Even though their captivity was fairly short - two weeks - the effects of the 'emotional maelstrom' are evidently long-lasting.' ***Professional Security Magazine***

'Linda reminds us that despite suffering horrible tragedies that we can and must move on with our lives and learn from our experiences. This memoir is an inspiring and uplifting read.' ***The Book Binder's Daughter***

'The story of her imprisonment and harrowing escape, which she has worked so hard in the past to forget, is told in candid and shocking detail. Crackling with tension, it is also laced through with black humor and insight. Iran is perhaps the most hated and least understood country in modern society and Linda's account gives a rare, illuminating glimpse into the realities of the oppressive regime.' ***The Gal in the Blue Mask***

Also by Linda Davies

Nest of Vipers

Wilderness of Mirrors

Final Settlement

Something Wild

Into the Fire

Ark Storm

Memoir: Kidnapped on the High Seas

For children: The Djinn Quartet:

Sea Djinn

Fire Djinn

Storm Djinn

King of the Djinn

Longbowgirl

To find out about Linda's latest books and news, please visit
www.lindadavies.com

To my husband, Rupert Wise,
love of my life, fellow traveller,
good in a crisis, and elsewhere.

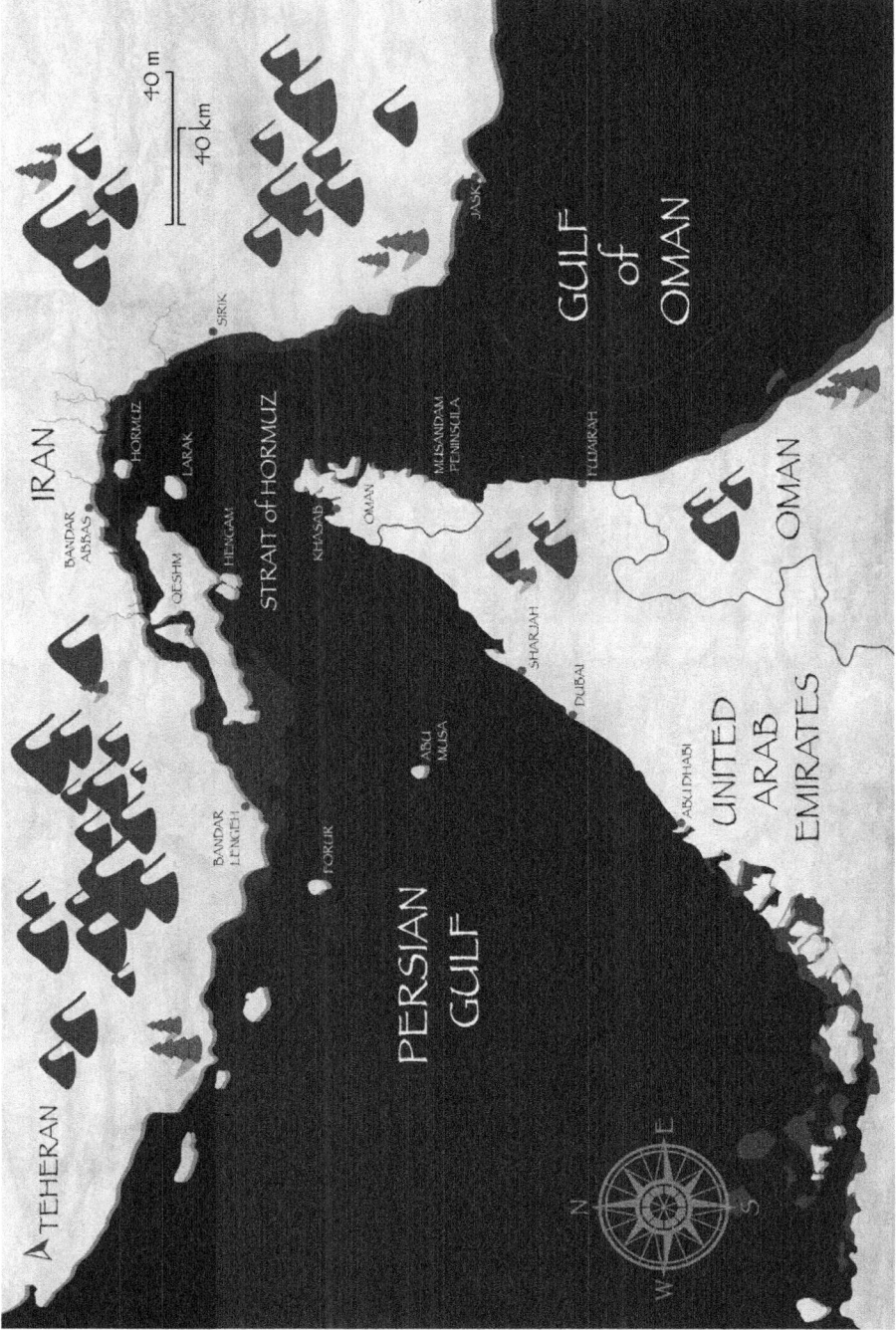

Linda, Rupert and their children at their Dubai home shortly before the fateful voyage

Linda in the Wahiba Sands in Oman

Rupert when he commanded the Sultan of Oman's desert reconnaissance unit

Rupert and Linda aboard another boat
in happier times

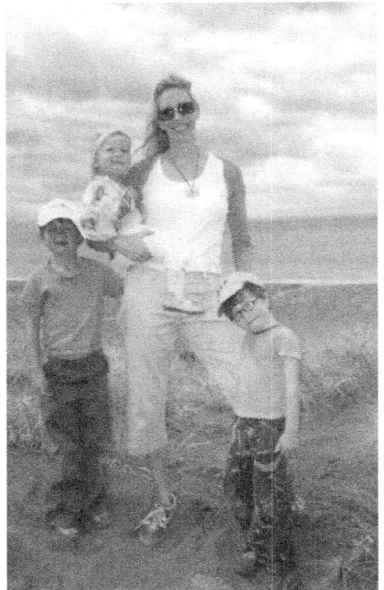
The family in New Zealand a few
weeks after their release

Prologue

I know it's all going horribly wrong when I see two gunboats approaching at full speed. They are bristling with men wielding Kalashnikovs.

Before they've even slowed to a stop in a giant wash of salty waters, armed men leap onto our boat. They are shouting and screaming and gesticulating with their weapons. Anything could happen. By design or accident. They are young, they are frightened and they are excited. They are out of control. I can smell their sweat.

Multiple thoughts race through my head: *This cannot be happening… they haven't put out fenders and the hulls of our boats are grinding together… they are stomping all over my lovely deck in their heavy boots… I really, really hope they have got their safeties on.* There is an air of malevolent unpredictability. This could go wrong very fast.

I glance at Rupert, my husband, and at Brad, our Captain. Rupert looks stunned. Brad looks scared. By mutual accord we all go still and quiet. I try to veil my fear. This is an animalistic situation. Showing terror or panic or provoking them in any way could push one of these volatile young men over the edge.

I covered up as soon as I saw the boats approaching but I'm still only wearing a bikini covered with a sarong. These men are in control of our boat. We are at their mercy. We have been boarded, an act of piratical aggression from time immemorial. It rarely ends well. We are two men and one woman far from home. No witnesses save the seagulls diving and wheeling above us, their afternoon slumber disturbed by the roar of the gunboats.

I know what language these men are screaming at me in. It is Farsi. They are from the Islamic Republic of Iran. *The Evil Empire*, according to popular demonology. We are British. We are their sworn enemies. We are their hostages.

Chapter One: Preparation

On a bright sunny day I was kidnapped at sea. You don't expect bad things to happen on beautiful days but they do. It's a long story. It also happens to be true.

This all took place some time ago. Long enough for the anaesthetic of time and distance to allow me to write this story with a measure of equanimity. It's fair to say I've actively avoided thinking about it over the years, but now it's time to cast back my mind and summon the memories... Autumn is the perfect time of year in the Middle East. The summer ferocity of the desert sun is muted to a rich warmth. The days are golden, the nights like indigo velvet. It's the time of year when all expats in Dubai thank their Gods that they are here and not back in rainy London, or urban New York, or grey Frankfurt, or damp Amsterdam.

We feel smug, like we got the game of chance right, like our Gods are smiling on us. First mistake.

It's Friday, the beginning of the Middle Eastern week- end. It's the last day of Ramadan, the Holy Month where practising Muslims fast during daylight hours. They break their fast when dusk falls, as defined by the impossibility of divining the colour of a thread. They are tired from the late nights when they stay up eating, weary of rising early for a predawn snack, enervated after days without food and water. The atmosphere is always febrile at the end of Ramadan. The roads become dangerous places. The incidence of fatal car crashes rises alarmingly.

My husband and I are off on a journey but not by car. It's 8 AM and the sun is already well up and the warmth of the day is upon us. We are in the Dubai International Marine Club. We are standing on the deck of a brand-new 38 foot catamaran we have named *Sinbad*. We are thinking how lucky we are to own such a beautiful boat. We are not sailors. We are fantasists, we are adventurers, we are adrenaline junkies (note to self: be careful what you wish for). We have very little sailing experience. But we have with us someone who does. We have a ship's captain, an Australian whom I shall call Brad. Who we don't have with us, *thank God*, is our three children.

Hugh aged seven, Tom aged four and Lara aged one, are all back in our home in Um Suqeim, a palm-treed oasis of villas and frangipani and carbon guzzling lawns. They are being cared for by our Nanny, an Australian I shall call Harriet. We don't want to take the children out sailing until we have tested the boat and gained more experience. Besides, this is going to be a two-day sail. Out to an island in the middle of the shipping lanes, mooring up overnight and back to Dubai the next day. When we do plan to take the children out we will go on very short voyages just for an hour or so. This is to be a grown-up adventure.

We are all organised. We have a massive lasagne defrosting in the fridge and a full bottle of Glenfiddich nestling in the icebox. We have multiple bottles of mineral water. I have told my good friend, Sarah Turner, a fellow British expat, that we are going sailing and that we will be back by 5 PM on Saturday. Just as an insurance policy, I told her that if I do not ring her by 5 PM then she is to push the emergency button.

Chapter Two: Setting Sail

The sun is shining as we manoeuvre away from the dock, past the gleaming super yachts. It is a still, be-calmed day. The flags in the harbour hang limply. There is not enough wind to hoist the sails. Motoring along is a bit disappointing but it is still a hell of an experience. The maiden voyage on our new boat.

We have two powerful engines and we cut along at about seven knots. We soon leave the futuristic skyline and the deserts of Dubai behind. We are now in a different world. The timeless passage of water that separates Dubai from Iran. A sea that was for many decades called the Persian Gulf but which is now known as the Arabian Gulf. Persian Gulf sounds so much more romantic to me. It conjures the wonders of antiquity, of *A Thousand and One Nights*, of Scheherazade weaving her tales before a turbanned tyrant.

Sinbad dances over the dazzling wavelets. We lose sight of shore. It is a strangely liberating experience for the landlocked. I know nothing about sailing. At this stage there is nothing useful I can do. I am totally in the hands of our captain.

I have had a busy week with my three young children and my writing. I have recently started a new book, a whole new genre for me. Young Adult fiction. I am writing a book called *Sea Djinn*. It is about three children's enthralling and terrifying adventures on land and at sea. They do battle with an ancient Evil Empire. But today the threads of storytelling float away from my mind as I begin to relax.

My husband stands at the bow of the yacht gazing out to sea. A handsome male figurehead scanning for lost islands and hidden treasures. A *Boy's Own* adventure. I am lying on the trapeze, a large square of rope netting suspended between the two forward floats of the catamaran. It is hot so I am wearing my bikini and my skin is soon tattooed with a latticework as if I'm waiting for a game of noughts and crosses to be played on my body. I lie on my stomach gazing down at the brilliant clear blue seas sluicing by beneath me. I think how beautiful it all is.

Where are we going? Well, to give you a bit of background, the Persian Gulf is a major shipping lane. Thirty five per cent of all seaborne traded oil flows through this waterway and out via the narrow Straits of Hormuz (where the shipping lane is just six miles wide). Mooring up overnight in this passage of water would be like pitching tent in the middle of the motorway. So we have chosen an island. There aren't many to choose from. There are the Greater and Lesser Tunbs. They are reasonably well known in the region as the subject of an ongoing punch-up between the United Arab Emirates and the Islamic Republic of Iran. Best avoided. But there's another island marked on the map. Marked with the symbol recognised by yachtsmen the world over: the international Mark of Safe Harbour. An island called Abu Musa. What none of us knows is that it is also subject to the same punch-up.

(Let's get this out of the way now: we should have known. We didn't. We were idiots. We didn't do our due diligence. It sounds a copout to say we relied on our Captain but we did. We shouldn't have done, to that extent. In mitigation, you don't board an aeroplane and interrogate the pilot. We were complacent and we made a mistake and we paid for it. Very nearly fatally.)

But back then, we sail blithely on, in a state of blissful ignorance. For the next few hours anyway… We have no idea what is awaiting us as we sail towards disaster.

Chapter Three: Abu Musa

We see the island of Abu Musa from a distance. It isn't very big, about twelve square kilometers, but it is hilly and it stands out in the endless expanse of blue. We have been at sea for hours and I am looking forward to mooring up and diving into the warm, clear waters. As we approach the island, my husband turns to me.

"Bloody hell, this place is tooled up!"

Bristling down at us from their cliff top positions are three anti-aircraft gun emplacements. We know it is a military base of some kind. What we don't know is that it belongs to the wrong side as far as international relations are concerned.

You might think that mooring up on a military island would be inadvisable even if they were on the same side as us, but there are many beautiful areas in and around the Emirates with military installations which happily coexist with tourists. There is one in the Musandam Peninsula in Oman, not far across the border from Dubai. It has a military base and it is a major tourist destination. The military and the tourists keep to their own sectors. You just know not to attempt to scale the razor wire. No harm is done. So for a few moments more we are still ignorant of what we are sailing into. Rupert and Brad are both excited by the prospect of mooring up here.

I feel deeply unhappy looking at the guns, but here's the thing. I don't want to be a spoilsport, I don't want to rain on the parade, I don't want to be a girl and say *oh my – guns! I don't like this, let's get the hell out of here.* So I stay silent. And my misgivings mount.

We sail closer. At first, there doesn't seem to be any sign of life but suddenly there is furious activity.

Then out come the gunboats.

Chapter Four: Gunboats and Kalashnikovs

The interrogation starts straight away. None of the men speaks particularly good English but a few of them can manage a bit. Gesticulating with their Kalashnikovs, they yell at us:

"Why are you here? Who are you? What you want?"

We try to explain. We are tourists. We are sailing a boat. We are on holiday. It is obvious they do not believe us. "Mobile phone! Give us phones."

Reluctantly, we hand them over. My phone is my lifeline to the other world. It is the thread that connects me to my children. Giving it away means cutting that thread. I have no choice. I hand it over.

"Camera!" they yell, eying my compact Samsung that sits on the table on the deck.

"Give camera!"

I give it to them. They look at it. It is not very sophisticated but I don't think they know how it works. They are getting very upset about the camera. It seems to be the focal point of all their anger and their excitement. I want to calm them down. I think they fear that we have taken pictures of the island. I want to reassure them. So I do something very stupid. For the right reasons I do the wrong thing. I open the back of the camera and I expose the film to the brilliant sunlight.

Now they really kick off. They scream at me. Their manic gesticulation goes up a few gears. I wonder if they will hit me. I quickly realise that, while from the perspective of the innocent what I have done is guileless, if I were guilty then what I have done is destroy evidence. It's all about perspective.

The hysterical interrogation continues. The sun begins to set. As darkness falls the atmosphere on the boat begins to change. For the worse.

Chapter Five: The Wrong Side

Night falls. This far from civilisation the stars are brilliant in the dark sky. There is light though. High-security beams shine out from the island of Abu Musa, cutting a golden path across the inky sea. It could look pretty if it weren't so terrifying.

The men are arguing, shouting, debating amongst themselves. The air crackles with tension. They fall silent. It seems like a judgement has been made, a decision taken. We are told to start our engines. We are told to turn around. With our armed escort, gunboat to the right, gunboat to the left, we motor away from the island.

In my novels I write about the metaphorical tightrope that we often walk unknowingly. On one side all is fine, on the other lies peril. I have now fallen off that tightrope onto the wrong side. It is as if I have walked into the pages of one of my books. Only here, I'm not in charge of the outcome.

My mind is racing. What's happening? What are they going to do with us? My logical brain answers my own question: we are either being freed or we are going to be shot and our bodies dumped over the side. The men have an air of grim intent. It feels and it looks from their expressions that we are about to be executed.

About 400 yards offshore, we are told to cut the engines. The men are becoming very agitated now. Their eyes dart back and forth. They glance at us, then each other. Their looks are horribly aware. They know something we don't.

They tell us to line up on the side of the boat. Hearts pounding, we do as we are told. What choice do we have? Dive into the sea and swim to Dubai?

Then the flanking boat behind us veers away and heads back towards the island. Out of range…

My husband and I look at each other. We know what the other is thinking. What a stupid way to die. It's not the first time I've had occasion to think that, but this time there really does seem no way out.

The men on the remaining boat form up opposite us. We are perhaps twenty feet from them. Easy targets… Armed with their Kalashnikovs, they cannot miss. They ready their guns.

Chapter Six: A Fate Measured in Seconds

Rupert and I look at each other. A last goodbye. What do you say when you think you have just seconds left to live? Standing on the deck, rocking slightly in the wash left by the departing gunboat, I feel an overwhelming regret, for messing up, for leaving my children orphans, for dying like this, so stupidly, so pointlessly. I look at the Kalashnikovs pointing at me and my husband and at Brad. I don't think of the bullets ripping into me. I think of my children. I fill my head with their faces. *I'm sorry,* I say to them, *I'm so sorry.*

And then the radios crackle into life. We hear shouted commands. The posture of the men changes instantly. They snap to attention. They lower their weapons, they click on their safeties. We are told to restart our engines. We are facing out to sea. We were about to be executed, now are we about to be freed? My emotions have gone into a zone all of their own, too extreme to process or to vent. I think it must be shock. I say nothing. I just stand in the darkness on the boat glancing at my husband and occasionally at Brad.

But then the men tell us to turn and motor back to the island. They order us to moor up on the pontoon. They tell us to wait. They do not tell us why. But we are alive and my heart pounds as if it is telling me: *I am here! You are here!* As if it knew that, but for seconds and the grace of God, we would not have been…

A plane roars through the night sky, coming in to land on the island. A few minutes later, two men in smart uniforms accompanied by three men in less smart uniforms materialise on the dock. These are men from the mainland. They are the superiors of the men on the island. They have come to decide our fate.

Chapter Seven: Interrogation

These men speak much better English than the island dwellers. It is not perfect but it is good enough. They are older than the other men. They are calmer. They do not carry Kalashnikovs but they are armed. Pistols nestle in holsters at their waists. I feel with them in charge we are unlikely to be harmed – at least not in the foreseeable future. Then I stop myself. What a ludicrous concept! The future is normally something we think we can influence if not control.(I'm well aware that this is not the case for many people. The ability to control our future is a middle-class, first world conceit, but it is one that is based on the very real power that we abrogate to ourselves via education, money and status.) But this is way outside my control. I really cannot foresee what is going to happen.

We are told to sit round the table. In a surreal parody of a social dinner, the men take their seats. The questions begin.

"Who are you? Why are you here? What is your business?"

And to me specifically: "Why did you expose the film? What pictures did you take? What did you see?" Over and over again the same questions. Over and over we give the same answers.

They are particularly exercised about the fact that our ship to shore radio does not work. They tell us in their calm, measured voices that the base on the island had repeatedly radioed asking us to identify ourselves, telling us not to come any closer, that if we did so we would be shot. Rupert and I and Brad exchange glances. How close had we come to being blown out of the water without even knowing it? While we sailed in towards the island, looking at the gun emplacements, men manning those emplacements were looking back at us. Like something out of a film Noir, we were in their sights without knowing it.

As I had stood in my bikini fantasising about jumping over the side and swimming, my body had been picked out in that circular scope. Head to toe, shoulder to shoulder, I had been standing in a ring of death.

But we had heard none of the requests, the demands, the threats. Viewed in that light our arrival could be seen as threatening. Again, it's all about perspective.

You would like to think that you had some sixth sense, some presentiment of ultimate peril. My instincts were kicking up, but the thing is you just don't think anything that bad can happen when you're brought up in our fine First World cultures. In our world, this sort of thing really does not happen unless you deliberately put yourself in harm's way, unless you go into the Armed Forces or the Security Services.

The questions continue. These men are Naval Officers and they cannot understand why our Captain could have put out to sea with a malfunctioning ship to shore radio. They seem to see in that negligence a deliberate conspiracy.

Middle Easterners are notorious conspiracy theorists. They thrive on intrigue. Perhaps it is the legacy of courtly rule and censorship. This leads to rampant speculation and foments a vivid imagination. And when you are the Evil Empire you are particularly paranoid. Most of the world really is out to get you.

The questions continue into the night. We are exhausted. Our defrosting lasagne lies sweltering in the heat. While we are being interrogated, our boat is searched by the island dwellers. They find our whisky. They display it triumphantly to our interrogators.

"What is this? Alcohol? You are bringing alcohol into the Islamic Republic of Iran?" demand the Naval Officers.

"This is not Iran!" we protest. "This island is owned by the United Arab Emirates!"

The men raise their eyebrows. Their lips twitch. They look vaguely amused. They do not engage in this surreal debate. Never has there been a clearer example of possession equalling ownership.

"It is an offence to bring alcohol into the Islamic Republic of Iran," they declare. "You are breaking the law."

It is obvious at this stage that they are looking for justifications to hold us hostage. Anything will do.

"We are not breaking the law because this is not Iran," I persist, perpetuating the fiction, at least in my own mind. They do not dignify my comment with a response. I ask them what they are doing with us. Rupert asks for our phones so that we might ring our embassies. The answer is a shake of the head. It is very obvious that the rules of normal engagement do not apply here. There is no phone call to a lawyer, no emergency call to an embassy. (Then again, in distressingly many cases in the bastions of Civil Liberties of the West, those calls are not permitted either. Though let me add, those imperfect democracies are a hell of a lot better than the alternatives.)

With instructions in Farsi to the island dwellers, the Naval Officers leave us, promising to return tomorrow.

Brad goes off to his cabin, Rupert and I go to ours and we lie in the darkness and we try to sleep while above deck the men with guns keep watch.

I think of my children. I think of them sleeping at home in their beds. They are safe and that gives me comfort. I wonder when I will see them again.

Chapter Eight: Badlands

We do not sleep that night. It is a relief when dawn breaks. It is another glorious sunny day. I should be diving off the side of the boat, swimming in the clear blue waters with my husband. Instead we just look at each other, each thinking the same thing. How could we have messed up so badly?

I drink water. We brought plenty of bottled supplies. We brew up coffee, offer some to our four captors. These men had drawn the short straw of the night watch. They look tired. I'm sure they were meant to stay awake and maybe some of them did but I suspect they snatched a few hours of sleep too.

They are young, maybe late teens and early twenties. They look like tousle-haired boys. Boys toting Kalashnikovs. Not so harmless. Yesterday they were ready to kill us.

Offering them coffee seems a civilised thing to do but some part of my brain also thinks it is a wise gesture of friendship. They look surprised, suspicious but I smile guilelessly as if to say, *don't worry, it isn't poisoned.* After a moment, with a quick exchange of glances, they take it gratefully. I drink my own coffee. I cannot eat.

The two Naval Officers reappear. The guards brush their hair with their fingers and stand straighter. They hop aside to allow the Officers to board. The two men acknowledge us with nods. They have brought a tripod and a video camera which they set up in our stateroom. Yesterday we were interrogated together. Today we are interrogated one by one and we are filmed.

They are the same questions over and over. Conscious that my performance will be viewed and picked apart by unseen eyes I try to make what is the truth appear as convincing as possible. *The truth will set you free…*

I have to believe it. I have the kind of face that shows my feelings. I am told that I am not good at veiling my thoughts and emotions. It gets me in trouble. I have nothing to hide but they do not know that. I have no idea how I come across.

The morning passes in a blur of questions. The Officers disappear, returning after lunch. They tell us that we are being moved. We are told to pack some things. I do not want to leave the boat. To do so means abandoning our way back. It means that we will be taken another step away from home, away from my children.

"Where are we going?" I ask. They do not answer me. This negation, this refusal to acknowledge let alone answer my questions is just the beginning of a process that makes explicit my own powerlessness. Knowledge is power, ignorance is weakness. They want us weak.

I brought very little with me for a two day sail. I pack most of my things. I have changed from my bikini and sarong into a stretchy, mercifully long black cotton dress. It has thin spaghetti straps which are wholly un-Islamic but if I wrap the sarong around my shoulders and tie it high I am reasonably covered up.

Some lucky instinct makes me pack Boggle, the word game that Rupert and I had fantasies of playing as the sun set with a glass of whisky in hand and the lasagne cooking in the oven. I also pack the various notepads that we had planned to use to record our words in the game. We walk off *Sinbad* not knowing when we will see her again. Led by the Naval Officers, flanked and followed by the men with guns, we walk along the wobbling pontoon and onto dry land. After a day and a night at sea it feels as if it is shifting under my feet.

We get into a car. We are driven along a dusty road through a barren wasteland, littered with the odd tumbledown stone dwelling, long since abandoned by the God-forsaken souls who lived on this island in decades past. Were they goatherds, farmers, fishermen? Hermits or ascetics? This is a sun-blasted, wind-scoured ghost of an island. It is not a palm-fringed, sandy beach fantasy, more an Alcatraz. It feels like the Badlands in a John Wayne movie from the 1940s. Nothing but sun and dust and doom. And gun emplacements…

We pull up at a landing strip. The plane that the Naval Officers flew in on yesterday sits on the tarmac. It is Soviet-era, propeller driven. It looks ancient, cobbled together. Which it no doubt is. Because of sanctions and Iran's inability to acquire new spare parts, it is more than likely the result of mass cannibalisation of other ancient, rickety, un-airworthy planes. Rupert swears under his breath. Yesterday, we avoided being shot to death. Twice. Now we will fly in a plane that looks as if it might drop from the sky at any moment. How many lives do we have?

"Where are we going?" I repeat. No response.

We board the rickety plane. The irreverent part of me that I often have trouble silencing pipes up inside my head: *Oooh, you've never been in a private plane before… you've never been in a military plane before… No,* I answer myself irritably, *and I have never been held hostage before. This is a day of firsts, isn't?* My irreverent self shuts up.

We fasten our seatbelts. The plane judders and bounces along the rutted tarmac. We take off and circle the island. I can see Sinbad below, looking ridiculously jaunty and incongruous. Part of me still cannot believe what is happening to us. How has it come to this?

We fly across the sea, over the dazzling Persian Gulf. It is obvious where we're going. We are bound for mainland Iran.

Chapter Nine: The Story Behind the Story

Let's back up a bit and start before the beginning. Notting Hill, London, 2002. Noon on a bright sunny day. Another bright sunny day… I have driven to see my publisher, Headline, in Marylebone. I have decided afterwards to go for a walk in Regents Park. We authors don't need to dress up most of the time, so though I was smarter than I would be for a day at my desk there was nothing ostentatious about me. Apart from my diamond engagement ring. It is a beautiful marquise diamond, several carats in weight. Like my wedding ring, I wear it everywhere. It doesn't occur to me to take it off. Maybe if I had, or if I had turned it round to hide the stone, I could have changed my fate, I could have avoided what was to happen next and the chain reaction it would set off down the years.

It is rare that we can pinpoint one, small inflexion point on which spins our destiny. Sometimes, in retrospect, we can and we wonder at it afterwards, at the power of that small moment, almost insignificant in itself. I've always believed in chaos theory: a butterfly flaps its wings and empires fall. This was one of those butterfly moments for my own life, though of course I had no inkling of it at the time.

So, wearing my ring, I walk in the park. There aren't that many people around. I often use walking as a way to dream up plots so half my brain is occupied with that but some little part of my mind becomes aware of someone somewhere, of the vaguest hint of threat. Maybe it is hindsight but I do remember a sense telling me to go back to my car.

I remember driving back to Notting Hill, pulling into my drive and glimpsing in my mirror a very scruffy car behind me and thinking (and forgive my snobbery here): God, that's a scruffy car for this part of Notting Hill.

My subconscious brain recognises that as an anomaly. Anomalies mean something if we can be bothered to think about them but I am in a hurry. I want to see my children, Hugh, aged four, and Tom, aged two (Lara hasn't yet been born.) It must've been a school holiday because Hugh was home instead of at school. I park my car in my drive, walk down the path to my back door which has a large glass panel in it. I catch sight of Hugh inside and I beckon him. I play peekaboo with him through the glass. I must have played it for a good few minutes. If I had gone straight in then maybe what followed would not have happened. Or maybe it would have happened another time with worse consequences. We can't second guess fate.

Suddenly down the path a man comes running at me. He ploughs into me. I start shouting. He tells me to shut up and to give him my ring or else he will stab me to death. On the other side of the glass, my petrified son watches. Alerted by my screams and his, my nanny, Jenny, rushes to the door. In panic she opens it. I cry out to her to close it. I do not want this man getting near my children. He is swarthy, lean and powerful. He has a twisted, hard face, void of any flicker of empathy or compassion. He is clearly habituated to violence. I like to think of myself as a fighter, but I'm out of practice and out of my league.

He punches me in the face, throws me into a wall and when I am dazed he struggles to rip the ring off my finger. I struggle back. It's instinctive. Who says our instincts are always trustworthy? He repeats his threat to stab me to death. He punches me in the face again and he rips the ring off my finger and he runs away.

That was the beginning of the end as far as my attitude towards living in London was concerned. My husband spent most of his time working in the Middle East so when Lara was born about a year later, moving to Dubai with our now expanded family seemed like an excellent idea.

In December 2004, we exchanged cold rainy London (which I still did love in many ways) for the warm balmy sun of Dubai which I soon came to adore. We all did. We put down roots quickly and decided within six months to extend our three-year posting initially by an extra year(we went on to stay for eight years).

Allow me to digress briefly and dismantle a little Shibboleth here. There are some people who say, *Dubai! How bling, how artificial...* They tend to be the kind of people whose own lack of imagination keeps them penned up in their five-star hotels or the glitzy restaurants or the shopping malls. There is another Dubai for those willing to step out of their air-conditioned cocoons. There is the vibrant Creek teeming with *abras* ferrying people and goods back and forth from new Dubai to old Dubai with its characterful merchant houses and meandering souks. There is the sea, turquoise-clear, home to a glittering kaleidoscope of fish, divine to swim in, wonderful to kite surf, periodically fabulous to surf. There are the deserts. You only have to drive for twenty minutes from the centre to enter another, much older world of sand and feather-leafed *Ghaf* trees, date palms and camels. There are the dramatic, serrated peaks of the Hajar mountains where you can climb the fabled Stairway to Heaven – a two thousand metre ascent up treacherous paths hewn into the baking rock. A day's drive away is the Rub' Al Khali, the Empty Quarter, beloved of adventurers and explorers from Bertram Thomas and St. John Philby to Wilfred Thesiger. Bordered by Oman, Yemen, Saudi and Abu Dhabi, the Empty Quarter is the largest sand desert in the world, with dunes the height of the Eiffel Tower and stars that gleam like diamonds. It is a harsh, other-worldly paradise – the ultimate antidote to the mall and hotel and restaurant culture. Thesiger, who crossed it and loved it passionately summed up its appeal: *"I knew instinctively that it was the very hardness of life in the desert which drew me back there – it was the same pull which takes men back to the polar ice, to high mountains, and to the sea."*

For the less adventurous, there are the rock pools at Hatta – beautiful cool oases of water fed by underground springs that are incredibly refreshing on a hot summer's day. All these other worlds are there for anyone prepared to get a bit sweaty. And we loved those worlds. They were a heady contrast to the urban life we had lived in London. Dubai, under the benevolent autocracy of Sheikh Mohammed and against the backdrop of moderate Islam, was a very pleasant place to live.

It was September 2005, we had been in Dubai for nine months, we were doing well and we thought it was time for a bigger adventure. I never spent the insurance money that came from the theft of my ring. I invested it instead. I did not want another ring. The old one had brought me joy, but it could have had me killed. I have never been overly bothered by jewellery and I thought there were better things to spend the money on. Like a boat!

(Buying the boat could have killed me too but of course I was blissfully ignorant of that at the time. What is the moral of the story here? That our possessions are not inert objects? That they can have a negative power? Or am I being fanciful and is it just a case of *stuff happens*?)

So we went to a yacht broker called Duboats and inevitably we were seduced. Our initial plans to get a small boat were replaced by more ambitious dreams and we ended up buying a 38 foot catamaran which we named *Sinbad*.

My husband and I had always been adrenaline junkies. After having children I became less so, but the lure of adventure on the high seas was strong and we thought we could have wonderful times in the Persian Gulf sailing *Sinbad* with our children. So a diamond turned into a boat and the dream turned into reality. And on a bright sunny day we set sail.

You might ask what we knew about sailing. The answer is not a lot but we believed we could learn. The Australian Captain, Brad, worked for the yacht broker and happened to be a supremely experienced sailor. As part of the deal he agreed to teach us. We would start with an inaugural voyage. The test voyage with myself, my husband and Brad. We would leave the children behind with my Australian nanny. We would only be gone for one night. I told my friend, Sarah, what our plans were, adding with a carefree smile that if we were not back by 5 PM on Saturday then she should sound the alarm.

I'm a novelist. I have a good imagination. I didn't even come close to envisaging what would happen next.

Chapter Ten: Be Careful What You Wish For

The rickety Russian-built plane begins to descend from the clear blue skies. We have not crashed.

Any such blessings are gratefully received. We come to a shuddering halt on a runway that is in shocking condition. We are escorted into a minibus, guarded all the while and we are driven off. The Naval Officers sit in front of us, more guards sit behind and upfront. Do they think we are going to bash the Officers over the head, commandeer the minibus and escape? The thought did occur to me, but where would we run to? Where would we hide? Who would harbour us? And how would we get off the mainland and back to Dubai? We would stand out horribly, we would be found quickly and we would be dealt with severely. This is Iran, a medieval theocracy with its hangings and beheadings, its stoning and amputations.

I push down all thoughts of escape and I look out of the window. I love to travel, I love to see other worlds. The part of my brain that is not horrified is curious.

We are in a coastal city, that much I divine, but I do not know what it is called. I desperately look for road signs but I can't see any. The first thing that strikes me is how rundown it is. Little square box houses, their whitewash stained and peeling; streets riddled with giant potholes and bordered by dust; ancient, drab, decrepit cars: most of them are small; most of them greys and dirty whites; most of them bear witness to multiple collisions. From what I have already seen of the driving here, that doesn't surprise me. Motoring can be adventurous in Dubai but the Iranians take road racing to a new and terrifying level.

There is one flash of glorious colour: a throwback to the glamour of a previous age. Standing out like thoroughbreds amongst donkeys is a succession of big old gas-guzzling American cars in gorgeous faded hues of sky blue, orange and pink. It is like a time warp. These cars must have found their way here during the regime of the Shah when America was Iran's closest ally before the 1979 revolution. So much has changed in the intervening years but still these cars roll on...

They give a hint of the legacy of wealth. No prosperity is visible now.(Of course to be fair it is possible that I am in the wrong town or in the wrong part of town but I will see more later that confirms me in my view.)

Just one hundred and forty five miles away, gleaming, futuristic towers pierce the skies of Dubai and Abu Dhabi while in their shadow lie marble palaces with palm-treed gardens. Driving around Dubai it often seems that almost every other car is a Ferrari or a Range Rover or a Lamborghini or a Porsche.

Iran produces three million barrels of oil per day. Where does that money go? Back in my life as I have already come to think of it, as if this were some kind of interlude between life and death, I have many Iranian friends. I think of them now and wonder what they would make of all this. Most of them fled Iran as very young children with their families after the deposition of the Shah.

When I was an investment banker one of my colleagues was Iranian. In the aftermath of the Revolution, his father was hanged. He bore no fond memories of the country. But other friends spoke wistfully of the beauty of Isfahan, of hiking through the snowy woods of northern Iran in winter, of the delicious food and even the wines that were produced in the Shiraz region before the Mullahs took over, imposed sharia and outlawed pleasure.

I had always wanted to visit Iran. Be careful what you wish for...

Chapter Eleven: The Safe House

We drive for about ten minutes then we approach what looks like a large naval compound. It has high walls topped by razor wire. In the corners are towers where armed sentries keep watch.

Out front there is a large gatehouse. Armed men stand on either side of a barrier. Another armed man steps out when he sees the car pull up. They all salute smartly when they bend down to the windows and see the naval officers inside. They look at me with thinly-veiled amazement. What is this woman doing here? I do not get the impression that there are any women in the Iranian navy. There's a short exchange and then the barrier rises and in we go.

We drive into the compound that in stark contrast to the world on the other side of the high walls is immaculately kept. The little box houses gleam with whitewash, the roads are tarmac not dust. There are pavements. There are even flowers and small patches of defiantly green grass. (It is military suburbia. With the benefit of hindsight my irreverent self thinks it looks like a down-market, militarised version of *Desperate Housewives* and *Wisteria Lane*, only all the inhabitants are male and all of them wear naval uniforms.)

We pull up outside one of the many whitewashed houses. We step out of the minivan. I breathe in deeply. The air smells of dust and cooking fires and exhaust fumes and something more exotic, a hint of fruity sweetness.

Before I can look around we are ushered inside and the door is locked. There are frosted windows with bars across them. Apart from that it is a perfectly nice house. It is clean and it is functional. It is the kind of place we might stay in if we were backpacking around Greece. In another life. It is not a prison. It would appear to be some kind of safe house.

Rupert and I are shown to a room that has four single beds in it. Will anyone be joining us? Brad is shown to another room.

An old-fashioned air conditioning unit blasts out frigid air. I shiver. In a masquerade of domesticity I unpack my pathetic collection of possessions: my sponge bag which contains toothbrush and toothpaste, lip balm, face cream and some tampons. They will come in useful but not for their designated purposes. On my bedside table I put a *Bertie* book by Alexander McCall Smith. Then I take out Boggle and the two notebooks and the two pens needed to play the game.

Rupert and I go back downstairs. Subconsciously we know we must maintain contact with our Captors. We must not languish in the room. We need to precipitate the next stage in this game. Whatever it is.

Downstairs the Naval Officers await us the in a dining room. They are sitting at the table. They stand up when we walk in. Away from our boat, away from the disputed island, on their own indisputably home territory they are somewhat improbably cast in the role of hosts. They ask us if we are comfortable. They ask us if they can get anything for us. I ask for our phones. I am denied but at least this time they shake their heads in acknowledgement of my question.

There is one other thing I would like. After many years of abstinence, I would like some cigarettes. Very much. My husband also thinks it is an excellent idea. What brand would we like, we are asked. Marlborough. There are no Lights but within five minutes a pack of Marlborough Reds arrive. They are handed over with a flourish. I smile and thank our Captors. They smile and give a small courtly nod. They are human after all. The irreverent part of my mind asks me is this Stockholm Syndrome or Stockholm Syndrome in reverse?

Chapter Twelve: The Veil

The doorbell rings. The Officers open it and admit two young men in uniform, clearly underlings as they are saluting furiously. This, I presume, is The Muscle, brought in to ensure we do not escape. There is a brief exchange in Farsi between the Officers and these new men. They sit at the table but they say nothing. They glance at me and then look away. They appear deeply uncomfortable, disapproving and vaguely puzzled. I soon find out why.

A few minutes later my Captors bring me another present: a *shayla* and a *chador*. Lest I forget it, I am now officially in the Islamic Republic of Iran and must dress accordingly, in 'good hijab'. This means covering my body, my hair, neck, ears and mouth, leaving just my hands, nose and eyes uncovered. Whenever I'm in the presence of any man other than my husband I must cover up.

I have always instinctively disliked these vestments, regarding them as a tool of oppression although they were worn in Dubai with a glamorous nonchalance by my Emiratia friends and with a studious rectitude by my recently radicalised Egyptian friend, Radwa.

Now I put them on with distaste. The *chador*, basically a floor-length, long-sleeved robe which fastens all the way down the front and comes up to my throat, is practical in some ways as the house is kept very cold and it keeps me warm but I thoroughly dislike the veil, or *shayla* as it is called in Dubai. I drape it over my hair and wrap it round my face so that it covers my lips. I immediately feel claustrophobic. It dulls my hearing, curtails my peripheral vision and cuts me off from the world. Is it intended to be a two-way barrier or just one-way? Is it meant to shield me from the predatory glances of males or to protect them from me? (There is a belief in Islam, based more

24

on culture than the Koran or the Hadith, that women, as the 'givers of life,' are more powerful than men and must be veiled for the good of society.) The shades of Eve permeate more than one religion… It's one hell of a back-handed compliment that I could do without frankly.

The Muscle sitting opposite me visibly relax. I am 'disempowered,' they are relieved.

I turn to my Captors. "So what happens now?"

"We talk some more."

Chapter Thirteen: Who am I?

This time we are interrogated separately. The officers set up the video camera in another room. There is a table on which it sits and three chairs. There is a bright light overhead but no beam shining into my face. Officer One and Officer Two, (I do not yet know their names) sit opposite me. Both men wear brown uniforms that probably aim for sand-coloured but hit mud instead.

Officer One looks to be in his late thirties or early forties. He is about five foot eleven with thick dark hair and the typical sallow colouring of the Persians but somehow manages at the same time to be a touch pallid. He looks like he doesn't get out enough and the tight waistband of his trousers suggests he enjoys his rice and kofta a little bit too much. He might have once been a fighting man but he looks now as if he would be most comfortable behind a desk. He is what I would call professionally hostile. He is not supposed to like me, or to be likeable and he is trying, I suspect against his better nature, to be vaguely unpleasant. Officer Two is about five foot eight, slim, fit and healthy-looking, probably in his mid to late thirties. He looks as if he would be more comfortable racing around on the deck of a ship, maybe springing up the rigging rather than sitting behind a desk. He too wears a veneer of professional hostility. I am after all, at the very least, a citizen of a country that Iran regards as an enemy.

Lights, camera, action: the questions begin. They are the same all over again: *Why did you go to the island? What were you doing? Why did you take photographs? What did you take photographs of? Why did you destroy the film? Why did you destroy the evidence?* The men take it in turns to ask questions. They lean forward, their bodies angled at me, their eyes hard, their voices aggressive. They are trying to intimidate me, to get me off balance so that I will make a mistake.

My answers remain the same. I am aware that I have to be consistent. Any deviations in my story will be picked upon and seen as evidence of guilt. They cannot believe our story, that we chose to 'holiday' at Abu Musa. You see, it's not one of those sun-kissed, palm-fringed fantasy islands that we all dream about. It's a lump of rock jutting out of the ocean in a strategically valuable location. Off the charts strategic.

Abu Musa is situated in the gateway to the Straits of Hormuz, through which travels much of the oil from Bahrain, Iran, Iraq, Kuwait, Qatar, Saudi Arabia and the United Arab Emirates: around *thirty five percent* of the world's sea-borne oil supplies. This is the most strategic strait of water on the planet. It is one of nature's finest choke points and it is controlled on one side by the Iranians, on the other, by Oman and the United Arab Emirates. At its narrowest point it is only twenty one nautical miles wide. Abu Musa could be used by Iran to harbour the gunboats tasked with blocking the straits with mines or even attacking passing tankers directly, thereby choking off global oil supplies and sending oil prices skyrocketing. And we have to convince these same Iranians that we visited Abu Musa only to swim, sunbathe and spend a quiet night.

So I painstakingly give the same answers, looking into the camera, wearing my veil, trying to make sure I look guileless and guiltless.

Who are you, the men continue to demand. *Why did you come to the island?* I realise that before they confirm or solidify their ideas as to who I am, or who I might be, I need to paint a very strong picture for them, one that will satisfy them and whoever it is who will watch the recording of the interrogation.

So who am I? How many times do we get asked that in our lives? I don't think I have ever been asked it before. What do you do, yes. What books do you read, what food do you like, what hobbies do you have, are you married, do you have children, where are you from? All of those, yes, countless times, but who *are* you? Never.

So here we go. This is who I think I am. I'm a woman pushing 40, who is married to a man, I have three children, stab in my heart, who are all very far away across the sea in Dubai. I have a Welsh father, now dead, and a Danish mother, very much alive. They met during the Second World War when my father went to liberate Denmark. They fell in love quickly but he was redeployed back to the UK. After a two-year, long-distance courtship conducted by letter, he returned to Denmark and married my Lutheran mother, a beautiful and statuesque red-head with a temper to match, taking her from her close-knit but relatively liberal farming community to the Pentecostal cloisters of the Welsh valleys. Talk about culture shock.

I am also a sister. I have three lovely big brothers – Roy, John Eric and Kenneth.(John Eric since died aged 58 of prostate cancer but that is another story). I was born in Scotland on the outskirts of Glasgow and moved aged four to a small house a pigeon's flight from the Welsh valleys. My father, since marrying my mother, had put himself through a series of menial jobs by day while studying by night and had gone on to become a teacher and then after more studying, an economics professor. My mother brought up her four children, looked after the home, bubbling with wit and humour and occasionally boiling over with the bitterness of unmet ambitions. At her school in Denmark, she gained the highest marks ever achieved and in other circumstances would have gone to university. But the Great Depression had forced her parents to sell their small farm and afterwards the family lived for many years in rooms in a house without running water. Earning a living took precedence over education which, in any case, seemed a bit of a luxury when living under German occupation. So my mother took a clerical job with an insurance company. Then, after she got married and moved with my father to the UK, the ethos and restrictions of the social milieu in which she moved and the exigencies of family life on a budget meant that all doors to a career were closed to her.

My grandfather on my father's side had been a coalminer in the valleys of South Wales. My father had used his considerable brain to escape that punishing life. There is a high premium put on academic attainment in our family but strangely we children were never pushed intellectually. We were, however, expected to be tough physically and emotionally.

I was a pony-mad tomboy who was brought up just like a boy, which suited me fine. I was expected to manage the same physical feats of prowess as my brothers: climbing mountains, swimming in cold seas, hiking in all weathers, indulging in a series of sibling competitions as to who could do the most pull ups, press ups, sit-ups etc, all whilst never complaining. Tears, unless the injury was life threatening, were met by a 'stop snivelling or you'll get a clip round the ear.' Don't get me wrong, it was a very loving household, but there were boundaries and tolerances born of fighting, enduring and surviving a World War.

My father bought me a longbow when I was eight and whenever the weather was dry and after I had seen to my pony I would go out and shoot Coke bottles lined up on a wall with my brother, Kenneth, six years my senior. For diversion, in the occasionally idiotically creative way of children, we would shoot at the high wire on the electricity pylons. Fortunately our aim failed us.

My father, a traditionalist in many ways, was an early feminist. As far as he was concerned his daughter could and should do anything his sons did. I was allowed vast freedoms, exploring the forests behind our house from the age of four and when I got my surefooted Welsh Mountain Section B pony, Jacintha, I would ride off just after dawn and roam the Welsh mountains for the whole day armed with a packed lunch in my saddlebags and a riding crop which I never had to use on my pony.

I grew up self-reliant and resilient. Qualities I was to be very thankful for.

I worked hard at my school, Y Pant Comprehensive (it means 'The Hollow,' in Welsh) and was overjoyed to win a place at Oxford University to read Politics, Philosophy and Economics. Using that as a stepping stone I got a job as an investment banker. Not a very noble calling, I know, but I had a plan. I stuck to it for seven years, long enough to make my running away money. Investment banking bought me freedom to write. And writing is what I had always wanted to do. It was my childhood ambition from as far back as I can remember.

So here's what I write: thrillers about the collision between the financial world and the intelligence world. My heroines are undercover agents in one form or another. My books are peppered with terrorists, counter terrorists, black ops specialists and spies.

And that of course is the great big elephant stomping through the room, the word which for some reason the interrogators are dancing around, not voicing but implying with every single question they ask: spy!

This last bit of who I am… This is not good. The word *spy* cannot be allowed to appear anywhere in the story of my life, even in a fictional capacity. At the best of times, people tend to think that novels are often thinly veiled autobiographies. My writing is a truth best kept hidden. Thereby illustrating an interesting point: even the innocent have secrets and lies…

I am not a spy. But in order to convince my captors of the truth, I must lie. It is not too big a lie. Perhaps you could say if you tolerate euphemism that I am merely massaging the truth.

I need a new, safe, wholly innocuous persona, close enough to the truth to be sustainable, so I tell them this:

"I write stories for young children, you know, stories of dolphins and birds and the adventures of little children. I have children you see and I like to write stories for them."

I think I can get away with that because my passport says I am Linda *Wise* whilst my writing name is Linda *Davies*. I have always believed that the separation between my writing identity and my domestic one was a good idea. I thank God for it now.

It is time to play my trump card, to win just a bit more sympathy from my interrogators and to start a piece of active misinformation that I am rapidly realising to be essential. "And of course, I have to look after my husband!" I say piously. "You see, he has a very important job." I wait a beat then I look into their eyes as I announce: "He is a banker!"

I realise that if they want to know who I am then they are certainly going to want to know who my husband is, what he does for a living. What he used to do for a living. And I know that if they find that out then we really will be in trouble.

Chapter Fourteen: *The Banker with a CV out of a Spy Novel*

After we were released, that is how my husband was described in the headline of a somewhat unfortunate article in the *Daily Telegraph* newspaper. My husband is a kind of banker, that much is true. But let me get this out of the way now. Apart from a short stint before he went to university, my husband never has been a spy and was not at the time of our capture a spy. Nor has he been since.

I do recognise that his profile would suggest otherwise and I'm aware of the mythology whereby the wife is always the last to know but profiling is a guide, not an infallible science, and I'd like to think I'm not so easily duped. With his background and his particular array of skills, my husband would have made a very good spy had he elected to take that route but he made a very conscious choice not to. The way he puts it, his family have worked for one hundred and fifty years in Government and Imperial Service and enjoyed exotic and wonderful lives but on retirement have ended up living in genteel poverty. He wanted a different life for himself and his family. He needed to make money.

Even though on the surface our backgrounds are very different, many of our core characteristics and driving motivations are almost identical. I wanted to make money to escape from the bonds of domesticity, not to suffer the periodic regrets and disappointments of my mother. Rupert was driven to make money so that he could establish the kind of life his family had once lived and now could no longer. And so he, like I, became an investment banker.

But finance is his second career. His background and his earlier career are rather more exotic. If he didn't exist, I'd have had to make him up and stick him into one of my books. He was and is the handsome, brave and dashingly manly romantic hero. In my fanciful moments I wondered if perhaps I had conjured him…

Rupert Wise was born in Al Mukalla in the Hadramaut region of South Yemen. That is where the Bin Laden family hail from. That is where many Al Qaeda terrorists hail from. Mukalla is an 'alert' word at the listening posts at GCHQ and at NSA. It is a red flag in a passport. Every time Rupert lands on US soil he fears a body search…

His father was a colonial administrator. His mother was a ferociously competent partner and help-meet to her husband and at thirty nine a surprised and delighted mother of an only son. She had a daughter, Myfanwy, nineteen years earlier by her first husband and had not expected to have more children. She doted on him but in no way smothered him. Rupert's upbringing in the wilds of Arabia was in one more respect weirdly similar to mine in the valleys of South Wales. He was given a massive amount of freedom. His favourite pastime was roaming the endless beaches on his donkey for hours, which he did from the age of four. There were no English boys to play with but he befriended the local boys and grew up speaking perfect colloquial Arabic.

His formidable mother educated him at home until he was seven but then she decided that he needed more than she could give him single-handedly, so she and his father took him back to the United Kingdom to begin a proper British education at a boarding school in the idyllic surroundings of Savernake Forest in Wiltshire.

Hawtreys had once been the ancestral home of Lord Cardigan. It was a beautiful and extremely grand house surrounded by eight thousand acres of ancient forest. There Rupert learned to box and to go 'rhodo-bouncing' with the other boys in the high canopy of the giant rhododendrons (basically hurling themselves like lemur monkeys from one large leafy bush to another) and to play dare with them in the deer park surrounding the school when the stags were on the rampage in the rutting season. He was a young boy far from home and he missed his parents and Arabia but he loved the new adventures of his Swallows and Amazons existence.

He was a bright and ambitious boy and at eighteen he won a place at Cambridge to read History. But before he began his studies, he did a number of unusual jobs. He worked as a roustabout on the North Sea oil rigs, two weeks on, two weeks off, and during the off time he worked at the onshore pipe yard facilities. After that he spent four months in the desert living with the Bedu, working for something called the Oman Research Department. It's an open secret that the ORD is basically an intelligence agency.

Back in Cambridge, the lure of Arabia resurfaced and he switched to reading classical Arabic. He got a Cambridge blue in boxing, captaining the winning side against Oxford in 1979. Pugilistic, skilful, and powerful, he never lost a fight. He graduated with an excellent degree and went straight into the army, to Sandhurst where he qualified as an officer (and went on to box for the Academy as well. He could have gone professional, but nice middle-class boys like him were not supposed to make a living thumping other people in the face). There followed a stint in Germany for the 14th/20th King's Hussars, a main battle tank regiment whose job it was to get flattened and to delay the invading Soviet Third Shock Army according to the paradigms of the Cold War and the perceived conflicts it might spawn.

But again Arabia called to him, and with great joy he left the north German plains on Loan Service to the Sultan of Oman's Land Forces where he led forward reconnaissance units spending months on end in the deserts of Oman and in the rocky, monsoon-kissed southern mountain ranges where the frankincense trees grow.

During his stint in the army he qualified as an SAS Combat Survival Instructor, which encompasses advanced skills in Survival, Escape and Evasion and Resistance to Interrogation.

We are planning on surviving without resorting to combat. Escaping and evading is a wonderful idea but the odds are overwhelmingly against us. All that leaves is resistance to interrogation, a valuable skill that has to be exercised in such a way that it is invisible.

You see what I mean about his profile. I have to, at all costs, conceal my husband's background and solidify his profile as a banker. And nothing more. The Iranians are primed as a nation to be on the lookout for Zionist spies and assassins, for agents provocateurs of the Great Satan and the Little Satan insinuating themselves into their country to foment counter-revolution. Catching them or any proxies that can plausibly fit that bill, parading them, hanging them in the courtyard of Evin Prison is a useful diversion from the privations of daily life. Or just making them disappear if that is more politic. Lining them up on the side of a boat, shooting their bodies into the sea…

I have to lead the interrogators in the direction I want them to go. I have to make them decide what questions to ask and to do that I have to play upon their natural curiosity as individuals not as agents of the state. One of the many things we have in common as human beings is curiosity about how other people live (as evidenced by the success of reality TV shows). In the Islamic Republic of Iran, where there is no free press but instead a state-created mythology about the West, there is a particularly intense and poignant interest in how the other half lives. And that is what I need to play on. I speak about banking and I speak about money and then I sit back and watch the direction of the questions change. I am putting my trust in my own particular maxim that money will set you free…

Chapter Fifteen: The Trap

After several hours, my captors stand, ending my interrogation, at least for today. One of them rummages around in his briefcase and brings out three pieces of paper. He pushes them across the table to me.

"You need to sign these," he says.

They are written in the Perso-Arabic script of Farsi. Lots of lines of Farsi. They all look the same but it is hard to tell exactly.

"Why do I need to sign them?" I ask. "What do they say?"

There is a frown of impatience. I'm meant to be answering questions, not asking them.

"They say that all the information you have given to us is true," one of them replies tightly.

I think to myself that they must say an awful lot more than that unless Farsi is an incredibly inefficient language. "Look," I say. "I cannot read Farsi. Please can I just write this in my own words, in English? I will sign it then but I'm really not happy signing something that I cannot understand."

I have heard the horror stories where captives have been given prison sentences in Third World countries after signing their names to a confession that they never understood and never made. Signing this piece of paper scares the hell out of me. There's every chance it's a trap of some kind.

The Captors confer briefly.

"We would like you to sign the paper as it is," one says. I look straight back into his eyes. I want to keep this civilised, not confrontational. I want to stay on their good side, as far as I can.

"Please bear with me, I cannot read Farsi and I'm really not happy signing something that I cannot understand," I repeat. "Please can I do it this way? After all, it's saying the same thing as you say is written in Farsi, it's just in my language. That's fair enough, don't you think?"

They do think it's fair enough. I can see it in their eyes. I capitalise on the moment and I begin to write on the first of the forms:

I, Linda Wise, do hereby declare that everything I have said during this interrogation, is the truth. And I sign *Linda Wise.* There was a moment when I nearly signed Linda Davies. My hand had hesitated briefly over the paper, but too briefly I hope for them to notice.

I turn the paper around to show them what I have written. I watch them reading it.

I find myself holding my breath. To my huge relief, they nod at each other. "All right. Do the same on the other two sheets," they say.

I write out two more copies of the same declaration and I sign each of them. I hand them back.

"Now you may go to your room," they say shortly. They are angry with me. I worry about that but I was not going to sign that bloody form in Farsi as it stood.

I nod and get to my feet. "Thank you. I'll just go to the sitting room for a while." I want to talk to Rupert and Brad. Quickly I tell them about the form and about what I had written at the bottom. I want us all to be consistent. I do not want any of us to trap ourselves. I don't get the chance to say anything more to Rupert because the Captors call him through for his own interrogation. Any attempt on my part to try and steer him away for a conversation would look inherently suspicious so I have to settle for a "see you later" and then take my seat on the sofa.

I know Rupert will not relinquish any information about his time in the Army but I can only hope that he too will maintain the fiction that he had been a banker since finishing university. I hope that he will not invent a different earlier occupation. I have been deliberately evasive about the dates and timings of his career, focusing instead on the insane salaries bankers are paid and the size of transactions in the City of London. I hid behind a persona that I have used often enough, generally advertently: that of the dumb blonde. They could not see my hair under the veil but blonde is more an attitude than a colour anyway.

They close the door behind them as they go out and then I hear the door to the interrogation room shut too. No eavesdropping is possible.

Brad says he is going up to his room for a lie down. I remain in the sitting room, alone but not unobserved. There is a hatch through to the dining area and a door that connects to it and every so often The Muscle walk by, always in a pair (do they think I could overpower one by himself ?) and check that I am still here. Not that I could go anywhere. All the doors are locked and all the windows are barred. They are frosted glass too so that no one can see in or out.

I sit in the sudden silence and time begins to weigh on me. I glance at my watch. What good is it to me here? I take it off. I would rather not see the agonisingly slow passage of the minute hand. I have Boggle, but you cannot play that alone and then I remember that I have Alexander McCall Smith. I run up to our bedroom, my feet pounding on the stairs, alarming The Muscle who come rushing out of the kitchen into the hallway.

"Book!" I say, coming down the stairs, brandishing McCall Smith like a passport. I walk past them, adjusting my veil so that all my hair is correctly covered.

I return to the sitting room and I dive into Scotland Street and the issues of *Bertie*, a precocious five year old with an overbearing, overprotective, over-controlling mother, Irene. The realities of life in genteel Edinburgh are the most blissful escape. I yearn for that world where the worst thing that happens is that Bertie is put into pink corduroy trousers by his gender-militant mother. As the minutes drag by, Alexander McCall Smith keeps me company. Mr McCall Smith, I thank you.

Chapter Sixteen: *Our Man in Havana* Comes to Bandar Abbas

Several hours later, Rupert comes through the door. I hear the Captors going to get Brad from his room. His turn with the video camera and the endless questions. Rupert and I are careful not to exchange any meaningful glances. By mutual, unspoken accord, we pare down our exchanges so that they cannot be misunderstood. But we do hug each other. We are big huggers at the best of times and an embrace between husband and wife in private is innocent, even in this culture.

We desperately want to talk but we feel sure that we cannot do so safely. So how to pass the time innocuously? The answer is Boggle. A word game comprising a square box with a lid, a base latticed with twenty-five little compartments into which a load of cuboid letters fall after being vigorously shaken. You then form words from contiguous letters, scribbling them down frantically in a race against the clock. The player with the most words of the most letters wins. So far, so innocent.

Or not. Our particular model causes an incident which gives some insight into the level of paranoia that persists. Some sets come with an egg timer to mark out the three minutes of each game. Our set however has an integral timer. We activate the timer by bashing the box against a hard surface. It then flashes red for about ten seconds to signify the start of the game. The Muscle, alerted by the banging sound, rush in to see what we are up to. They see the flashing box and start yelling. The Officers burst out of the interrogation room to see what is going on. Alarmed, they glance between us and The Muscle and the flashing box. They take a step back. Clearly they think it might be a bomb but are unsure because we are sitting here in a posture of relaxation. But then perhaps we are the coolest *shuhadaa* (martyrs/ suicide bombers) ever.

"It is a game," I say. "A word game."

The flashing has stopped. The Captors approach and study the box.

"Who are you communicating with?" they demand, turning back to us.

"Er…" Rupert and I look at each other, attempting to veil our disbelief. They don't think our Boggle is a bomb any more. They think it is a communications device.

Brad has emerged from the interrogation room. He is watching the proceedings with a look of incredulity.

"We are not communicating with anyone!" we say. "It is a game. Look, we will show you how it is played."

I close the lid and bash the game against the table. Warily, the men watch the pulsing red light. They see that it stops flashing after ten seconds. Both Officers are glowering at us and The Muscle is looking extremely nervous, clearly thinking that they have messed up big time. Then the Officers see the notepads. And it goes from bizarre to surreal.

Both notepads have been used by Rupert and me to record our words in countless games past. My notebook, however, was occasionally purloined by Hugh, my seven-year-old son, who has a thing about drawing islands. Our Captors flick through these pages with forensic interest.

"What are these words?" they shout. "What are these islands? Is this Abu Musa?" they ask, pointing at one particular drawing which is reasonably detailed and appears to show various points of ingress onto a mountainous island. "Why you drawing these islands?"

"These drawings are by my son. He is seven," I say.

"What are all these words?" they demand, gesticulating furiously at page after page of words. "What are these numbers? What code is this?"

"It is not code," we reply. "It is a game. The words are part of the competition. The numbers are the scores."

This does not reassure them in the slightest.

"We need to take these notepads and the flashing box," they say gravely. The shorter man takes it, somewhat gingerly, then they both walk out.

The door closes and I can hear one of them making a phone call. A few minutes later I hear someone come to the door. I guess he is taking the game and the books away to have them analysed, to try and break the code.

I don't think there is a cryptologist alive who could decipher a code from the words and the circles and the brackets and the numbers on our notepads. A three letter word gets one point, four letter words gets two points and so on. Words that are duplicated between players get crossed out. For purposes of speed, plurals are not written separately but 'S' is added in brackets at the end of the word, or if you can turn a noun into a verb then 'ING' is added in brackets at the end. You get the picture. To the uninitiated it could look like a very sophisticated code.

Part of me smiles to myself at the thought of the code-breakers who will be set loose on our notepads. It is almost Kafkaesque in its surrealism. It makes me think of Graham Greene and *Our Man in Havana* and the source/ spy who sends back to London, via his case officer, drawings of vacuum cleaner parts claiming that they are a secret military installation.

I suppose that to a hammer everything looks like a nail. To a repressive regime, which counts most of the West and much of the Arab world as enemies, everyone looks like a spy and everything looks like code.

Chapter Seventeen: *Maktoob*

Deprived of Boggle, I return to Alexander McCall Smith. Rupert has a book of his own too. *The Time Traveller's Wife* by Audrey Niffenegger. He loves reading but he's not enjoying this book even though it is well written. It is too discordant, too emotionally raw, too depressing. Its subject matter is somewhat ironic. If you asked me then if I would turn back time to the day before we set sail so that I could abort the whole voyage then my answer would be an immediate and unequivocal *Yes*. Were you to ask me now, nearly nine years on, I would not be so certain.

I have often witnessed the law of unintended consequences play out. I incline towards the theory that things happen for a reason. Certainly that mindset takes some of the fight and the bitterness out of life. In this part of the world, the belief in *Maktoob* (fate), is very powerful. When some years back, I gave my condolences to an Arab friend who had lost his son in a car crash, he gave a heart-breakingly eloquent shrug of pain mingled with acceptance. *"Maktoob,"* he said sadly. *It was written. It was his fate.* Events good or bad are put down to "God's will." There is the sense that there is little scope for individual determinism. There are notable exceptions. The Arabs used to say of Lawrence of Arabia that his fate was not written, that he was the master of his destiny in a way that most mortals are not. Whether or not you are religious, *Maktoob*, God's will, things happening for a reason, is a workable and comforting philosophy with, I suspect, a good measure of truth in it insofar as you can define such nebulous theories as true or untrue.

Perhaps this misadventure put us off sailing and saved us from something far worse at sea. And I did learn valuable life lessons. I suspect that with the hindsight of nine years I would have gone ahead with the voyage, even knowing what it entailed. But perhaps it is like childbirth. Perhaps I have forgotten the true horrors and the pain. Time is a wonderful anaesthetic.

So Rupert puts aside *The Time Traveller's Wife* and I read aloud to him and to Brad some of Bertie's escapades in Scotland Street. We find ourselves chuckling. The Muscle looks at us askance. Brad stays with us for a while but then goes back to his room to sleep.

Some hours later the Officers return.

"We have photocopied the notebooks," they say. "You may have them back." They hand them over. Their inherent sense of manners and hospitality cannot prevent them from smiling slightly when they give us things. "Here is your game." They return Boggle to us. Perhaps somebody in Headquarters is a demon Boggle player and has recognised the game. I can only hope so.

Now that they are fractionally better disposed towards us I ask again:

"Please will you let me talk to my children?" I look them straight in the eye as I continue. "We were expected back a day ago. If we do not call them they will think that we have had an accident at sea. That we are dead. Please let us call them."

They shake their heads. "Not possible," they say.

Chapter Eighteen: *The Last Samurai*

Our Captors ask if we would like to eat dinner. I have a tendency when very upset not to eat, but I know I need to keep strong and resilient and so I nod with the full intention of eating properly as do my husband and Brad.

In the meantime, Rupert and I smoke. And then we smoke some more. Anything to pass the time, to occupy and distract us. *Whatever gets you through the day...*

We are now in the midst of the Eid holiday – the celebrations to mark the end of Ramadan. None of the major decision-makers is likely to be at his desk (and in this country it will be a 'he'). We are hoping that when the holiday finishes the powers-that-be will review the video footage of our interrogations and come to the inescapable conclusion that we are blundering idiots, not spies. That is the horizon we look to in our minds and in our hearts. We will see our children in a few days. We pace ourselves for that. We can manage a few days of this, sure, no problem. We fixate on the end of Eid, pinning all our hopes on it.

The suffering of our children, not knowing where their parents are or what has happened to them, is something that can only be imagined. I do not know what they have been told. I can only hope that our nanny, Harriet, or my friend, Sarah, have invented some tame reason, have bought us time and granted my children peace of mind.

A new team of Muscle arrives to relieve the first lot. They look delighted that we smoke and light up themselves. We sit in a fog of cigarette smoke. Poor Brad is by default a heavy passive smoker. Half an hour later, dinner arrives. Chicken kebabs, rice, unleavened bread and okra. It is a good meal. I cannot fault my Captors' hospitality. I have no appetite but I force myself to eat.

Then in a bizarre twist, Officer One asks us if we would like to watch a film. We nod eagerly. The Officers say goodnight and The Muscle sets up a video of Tom Cruise in *The Last Samurai*. I've seen it before and loved it and ended up crying profusely as I often do irrespective of whether films are happy or sad, much to the amusement of my children. Curtains are drawn across the barred windows, dinner is cleared, night falls.

Rupert and I sit together on a small sofa, Brad sits in an armchair and The Muscle perch on chairs pulled in from the dining room. We settle down together to watch Tom Cruise. Dubbed into Farsi. It is a badly pirated video. It is wonderful. It fills my head and it blanks out some of the pain. Tom Cruise, I thank you!

Chapter Nineteen: Bandar Abbas

Rupert and I are exhausted but we toss and turn for hours. Finally we fall asleep in our single beds, tucked up against the freezing air conditioning under several layers of fleece blanket. The next morning, we create an opportunity to talk properly. We take a shower together. We suspect that our bedrooms and everywhere apart from the bathrooms have been wired for sound and possibly vision. We fervently hope the bathrooms have not been bugged but we cannot assume that.

Even if they have, the running water will mask our conversation in a manner that is not nearly as inherently suspicious as conferring behind closed hands and shut doors. We hold each other, standing under a mercifully hot torrent of water, whispering into each other's ears like lovers. Only these are no sweet nothings. These are plans to secure our release.

I tell Rupert of my banking plan, my money plan to distract our Captors from the true back story. Rupert luckily has stuck to the investment banking theme wholeheartedly as well and has not invented a replacement earlier career for his army background. We also agree that I should be the one to take the forefront in communicating with our Captors as I am likely to be able to gain more advantage. Also the further they are kept from Rupert the better.

Next in the order of business. Where the hell are we? "I'm almost 100% certain we're in Bandar Abbas," whispers Rupert.

"How do you know?" I whisper back.

"Because in the '80s there was something called the Musandam Development Corporation, a.k.a. the CIA. All of us in the military knew about it. They had a listening post at the tip of the Musandam Peninsula, getting Sig Int on Bandar Abbas. It's a mainland port with major naval and air force bases, a strategic choke point for the Straits of Hormuz," he explains. "Plus I looked out of the window on the plane at the direction we were going in and the time it took us to get here."

I love my husband! My father had an uncanny ability, born of his curiosity and a near eidetic memory, to be able to answer just about any question I put to him. My husband is the only man I've met since who even comes close. I feel a small sense of euphoria. We know something that they don't think we know. Somehow we will use it to our advantage, I just don't know how yet. Throughout my life, knowledge has been currency. I trust it will continue to be so.

We emerge from the shower and I violently towel dry my hair to keep from getting a chill. Last night I hand washed my underwear as I do not have multiple changes. I pull that on, and my black dress, a thin cardigan and my chador. I arrange my veil. At least it keeps my head warm. Always a silver lining…

We head downstairs. Brad emerges looking unwell, pallid skin but red cheeks. "It's my blood pressure," he says. "I can feel it rising." We chat about how we are but we are all feeling the strain. We are hopeful, we are fearful, we need to convince our Captors of our innocence. We are all trying to keep up morale.

The night team of Muscle is relieved by the day team who bring breakfast. Unleavened bread, oranges, cheese, jams, and coffee. It's a pretty good breakfast considering. And more cigarettes. We are smoking a lot.

The Officers arrive and bid us good morning.

"How are you? Did you sleep well?" I am familiar with *Tarof*, the concept of civility and politeness that used to be ingrained in the Iranian psyche. Post-Revolution, it is seen by many, the hardline clerics and their Basij henchmen in particular, as a sign of weakness. These Iranian men possess it, thankfully. We will come to meet others who do not. So we answer politely and inquire in turn after their own welfare. With the niceties over, the interrogations can commence.

I continue to answer the questions, I continue to talk about money. I continue to request access to our Embassy. I continue to ask for permission to ring my children. Both requests meet with a pursing of lips and a shake of the head.

"No, not possible."

"What about the Geneva Convention?" I ask. I really don't know much about it, but I suspect there must be something about access to Embassies. But then, Iran is a pariah state, it does not play by the international rules. It made that much clear by snatching us from what are patently the territorial waters of the United Arab Emirates according to international law. Why should I expect them to start respecting international law now? However, there is another law that they do respect and it is to this that I decide to appeal.

"Are you married?" I ask them. They look surprised and say nothing. I am only just getting started. "Do you have sisters?" I continue. "Do have daughters?" They glance at each other, puzzled and discomfited by my line of questioning.

"You have mothers. That much is for sure!" I declare. This is met by faint smiles. Clearly they wish to impart no personal information but this much is undeniable.

Anyone who has lived in the Middle East knows how much they value family and how in Islam the family is sacrosanct. And Iran is after all a highly Islamic country with religion an integral part of its national identity (the grip of the Revolutionary Guard and the Islamists on the country is loosening, as evidenced by the historic handshake with the United States and the nuclear deal. But that is another story, nine years in the future).

But Iran is much more than an Islamic revolutionary state. It is an ancient nation, rich in culture and history. The Iranians are very proud of their heritage. They do not regard themselves as Arabs. They see themselves as hailing from an infinitely more sophisticated culture than what they refer to as the 'camel jockeys' across the Gulf, meaning the citizens of the United Arab Emirates, Qatar, Bahrain, Kuwait, Oman and Saudi.

It is to that sense of identity coupled with strictures of Islam that I now appeal. I lean forward, scrutinising them both. "You are civilised men," I say. "You are good Muslims. Is this how you treat your women in Iran? Is this how you treat your wives, your mothers, your daughters, your sisters? Do you think this is right what you are doing, keeping me from my children? Keeping my husband from our children? Not permitting us to even telephone them? How would you feel if I were your wife? You would want me freed with my husband and with Brad, immediately."

They shift in their seats. They look pained.

"How can you do this? How can you continue to hold us? You know we are innocent. When will you let us go?"

"Don't worry," they say to me, "you will be free soon.

You must just answer our questions, then you will be free."

"When?"

"Tomorrow. Maybe. *Inshallah.*"

The Eid holiday that marks the end of Ramadan is almost over. The decision-makers will be back at their desks tomorrow. Maybe tomorrow, we *will* be freed. *Inshallah.*

Chapter Twenty: And Days Go By…

Tomorrow comes. We are not freed. We are interrogated throughout the day. It is exhausting and nerve-wracking but the periods when we are not being interrogated have their own challenges. How to keep yourself occupied? How to keep your emotions under control? How to control the lacerating pain whenever you think about your children and what they are going through, and when you will see them again? How to fill your mind with something else?

How many cigarettes can you smoke? How many times can you re-read Alexander McCall Smith, no matter how wonderful he might be?

Several more days and nights pass in a blur of interrogations and triplicate form filling, of cigarettes smoked, badly dubbed films watched, games of Boggle won and lost, meals consumed, Alexander McCall Smith devoured and, finally, the blissful escape of sleep.

The relationship with our Captors is evolving subtly. We are spending so much time with them that we are getting to know them a little and they are getting to know us a lot. They are at the house for around twelve hours every day, interrogating us, or sitting and occasionally chatting with us whilst they wait for their mobiles to ring with instructions or more questions from the invisible eminence gris (or eminences) who is very evidently pulling their strings.

My interrogations cover all the same questions which I answer as if by rote. I explain for the umpteenth time why we came to Abu Musa, why I destroyed the film in my camera, why our ship to shore radio did not work, and who we are. But every so often a new question, possibly from the Dark Eminence, is dropped in: Did we tell the Dubai Coast Guard about our voyage? Did we give them the plan of our voyage? I'm not sure of the correct answer and so I tell the truth even though it sounds suspicious. "No," I say, "I don't think we did."

"What do you mean, you don't think you did?" they ask with either real of feigned anger, I cannot tell.

"Well, let's put it this way," I reply. "I know I didn't because I wouldn't know who they are or how to get in touch with them. And I know that Rupert didn't because he didn't mention doing it. Brad might have done it but if he did do it he didn't tell me, so I would have to assume that we didn't tell the Coast Guard." I'm aware of the possibility of somehow tripping myself up, of saying the wrong thing, of revealing something that would compromise us in some way. To a conspiracy theorist picking over the videos of my interrogation, it is possible that any small throwaway remark could be seen as incriminating. I am well aware that it sounds inherently suspicious that we did not tell the Coast Guard of our plans. It makes it seem as if our jaunt were in fact a dark voyage, under the radar, clandestine, a spying mission... You don't have to make much of a leap to get there. I have to be careful. I always have to be careful and keep up my guard. But when you are exhausted, and when you are lulled into potentially a false sense of security by the repetition of questions, it becomes dangerous. I know enough to realise that it is meant to be.

Often during my interrogations I start pouring with sweat. I am grateful then for my veil and for my chador as it conceals my sweating, as it covers up the muck sweat of my fear. The interrogations are the only thing we can do to influence our fate. Nobody from our Embassy knows where we are. We are lost in Iran. At this stage, only we can fight to secure our own release. Our freedom hangs on the interrogations. Watching my children grow up depends on them. The stakes could not be higher.

Wherever possible I digress to discuss how much money bankers make and how absurd is the price of property in central London. And then when the interrogation winds down, when the interrogators begin to run out of energy, I appeal to them as Muslim men, as family men, to release us all back to our children. (Brad too. I am very careful to stress that we come as a package of three.)

With every hour, with every interrogation, I keep hammering home the Iran/ancient culture/Islamic/family theme. I feel that I am establishing a deepening bond with the Captors. I will not stop until I'm convinced that they see me not as a spy, not as the travelling companion and wife of a spy, but as a mother, a sister, a daughter.

I think they are increasingly coming to believe that we are all innocent. I sense a shift and I believe that they are now on our side. These men who were originally so hostile have warmed to us. They buy us cigarettes. They even buy me lotions and potions from the chemist. They are quite plainly good men. I sense that they are our advocates.

They are charmed by Rupert's new pastime. He is memorising and reciting Arabic *surahs* (chapters) from the Koran that lies on the table. He does this to pass the time and to keep his head occupied, but our Captors, whom I shall name Reza and Ali, are seriously impressed by his knowledge of the Koran and his interest in it.

They are clearly receiving instructions on their mobiles from the Dark Eminence telling them to keep on interrogating us possibly in the belief that we will break. It is equally clear that they themselves do not think that we will break. They think there is nothing to break, that our stories are the truth. That nothing sinister lies beneath the shell of who we say we are.

Chapter Twenty One: A Phone Call

Finally, we get a breakthrough. After five days, they allow us to telephone our children. We are in the sitting room, between interrogations.

Reza and Ali come in, carrying two briefcases. They spin the combination locks, open the cases. Reza pulls out my mobile, Ali withdraws the battery. They reunite them. Ali, the older, taller one tells us:

"You may speak briefly to your children so that they know you are still alive. You will tell them that you are having engine trouble and that you are trying to fix it."

I nod enthusiastically. I will say just about anything they like as long as I can talk to my children. This severance has felt like an amputation. This yearning is unlike anything I have ever felt before. I am physically incomplete, bereft of them, of their voices, of contact of any sort.

They hand me my phone. I feel my spirits lift. The phone is my lifeline to my children.

The Officers stand behind me as I dial the home number. I can tell very quickly that my phone has been gone over. The configurations are different. What I hadn't anticipated was the difficulty of placing the call from Iran to Dubai. The networks are busy. I could weep with frustration. I am desperate to hear my children's voices and to let them know that I and their father are okay.

I cannot dial last number recall for some reason. Instead I have to tap out the numbers individually over and over again in my attempts to get a connection. Our Captors stand behind me watching me all the while, looking over my shoulder. Finally after about ten minutes, I get through.

Our nanny, Harriet, answers. I say, "Hello, Miss Harriet." I never call her that. She is always plain Harriet. I hope that she will infer from this that we are in trouble. I ask how the children are.

"Well, they're wondering where you are and what's happened to you and Rupert." I contemplate telling her what has happened, rushing out the words, but I do not. My Captors would grab the phone in seconds and then I would not have the chance to talk to my children and at the moment that is all and everything that I want to do. Also, I do not want our children to know what is happening to us. I do not want to shatter the security of their world any more than it might already have been, depending on the fictions they have so far been told by Harriet or Sarah. I need to get word of our capture to our Embassy, but there has to be a better way. So I ask to speak to my children and Harriet goes and gets them. I hear their voices as they approach the phone. My heart beats faster. I have a visceral need to speak to them that dominates my mind and my body.

I have never been much of an actress but I have to call upon all of my limited talent now, and all of my self-control. Most mothers regularly have to cover over adult problems or sadness and fake a jollity they do not feel for the sake of their children. I am reasonably adept at that but this is a whole other order of magnitude. I hold the phone in my right hand and I dig the nails of my left hand into my palm as hard as I possibly can and I paste on a smile as if they can see me and I speak to my three children.

I talk to them for about two minutes, asking them what they have been doing, maintaining the fiction of our engine trouble, explaining that we also had phone trouble which is why we hadn't managed to ring them and then my Captors signal to me to end the call.

"I love you," I tell them and I say goodbye. I end the call, give back my phone and then I double up, hugging my knees, hiding the emotion that wracks my body in silent sobs. At least I have spoken to them. At least I have allayed their worries. At least I have heard their voices.

Chapter Twenty Two: To Be Or Not To Be…
An Island

The Captors ask Brad if there is anyone he would like to call. He shakes his head.

"I come and I go. There's no one who'd miss me yet. I don't speak to my mother all that often and besides, this would scare the hell out of her. Duboats might be a bit suspicious about my absence though."

"You can't call Duboats."

They would not buy the fiction of *engine trouble*.

"No, I thought as much," he responds tartly. "So no one, thanks."

His response makes me think of the Francis Bacon quote, albeit intended to have a different meaning:

"He that hath wife or children hath given hostages to fortune."

Bacon meant that family ties were impediments to the achievements of the single man, but I read the power of the quote differently. When we love, when we create a family, the hostage to fortune is the safety and unity of that family.

I prefer John Donne's take on the human condition. *"No man is an Island entire of himself."* When we love, we create bonds, and they bring us untold joy. And on occasion, the sharpest pain. That is the price, but if you offered me a choice, I would choose the pain over the isolation every time.

(I think Brad would as well, as evidenced by his behaviour after we were set free, more of which later.)

That evening, as our Captors are saying their goodbyes, their "see you tomorrows," Brad raises an eyebrow and says with a lovely little sardonic lilt to his voice: "Yeah, tomorrow. We can have a party. Tomorrow is my birthday." This generates a complicated response on the faces of our

Captors. They look at once regretful and determined.

"Your birthday? Really? Then we must celebrate!"

"Yeah. It'd be nice to have something to celebrate," Brad replies with just a hint of anger. "Like our freedom."

"Inshallah," they reply softly. (Everything is *Inshallah* – if God wills it.)

Chapter Twenty Three: A Nightmare Birthday

The next morning Reza and Ali arrive bearing a chocolate cake. They turn and make a beckoning motion. Muscle One emerges from the kitchen with matches and lights the candles.

"Happy birthday, Brad!" say The Captors. Brad gives an eloquent smile of gratitude, pain, weariness and yearning. This was not quite the birthday he had had in mind. But he is gracious.

"Thank you," he says faintly as he blows out the candles. There are ten of them. Does that grant him ten wishes? We do not sing *Happy Birthday*. The irony would be too great. We just haven't got it in us and I think Brad would thump us were we to burst into song. We all sit down together for a small slice of cake. The pathos of it is almost too much.

I ask if I can call my children again, just to hear their voices.

"Yes, but you must say you are waiting for a spare part for your engine. That you cannot sail back yet."

I nod. "Fine. I'll do that," I promise them. How ludicrous is that cover story anyway? *Sinbad* is a sail boat. All we need is wind… But I'll say whatever I need to say to keep contact with my children.

Reza and Ali disappear to wherever they are keeping their briefcases, some safe I imagine, and return a few minutes later. They unlock their cases and assemble my phone. They hand it to me and stand behind me.

I take a few breaths to compose myself and then I dial. No connection. The international networks are busy. I try for another ten minutes with no luck. My Captors move away and sit down, mild impatience in their eyes.

"Please, just let me try for a few more minutes."

They nod. I keep trying. I get through. I hear those lovely high-pitched voices, clear as bells across the ocean. They are all fine. Of course they ask when we will come home. "Soon," I say. "We're still having engine trouble. Waiting for a spare part," I add.

My Captors stand up and approach, signalling at me to end the call. "I have to go," I tell them. "I love you…"

I hand back my phone. They disassemble it, take away my lifeline.

That evening, after another exhausting day of interrogations, our Captors return after a brief absence, smiling in delight.

"We have good news for you! We have a birthday present for you, Brad. We have a present for you two as well!" they declare, looking from me to Rupert.

My heart starts to pound. *Could this be it? Please God,* I think in my head. *Please God.*

And then I hear the words, the words I have been craving.

"You. Will. Be. Freed. Tomorrow. *Inshallah.*"

We beam at them in wonder. I reach out and shake their hands with delight. Tomorrow we shall see our children! Tomorrow we shall be free! My soul bubbles over with joy. I see in Rupert the same rising delight, the same flowering of hope into belief.

"Yup, that's possibly the best birthday present a guy could ask for," declares Brad.

Chapter Twenty Four: Sins and Transgressions

Tomorrow comes. We awake and jump out of bed, filled with a sense of purpose, bubbling with a latent euphoria. Today we will be freed! We dress quickly and hurry downstairs. Our Captors arrive. Rupert I move to shake their hands. Their reaction is immediate. They step back as if I have the plague. They look at me apologetically. Ali explains. "It is forbidden under Islam for you to touch any man outside your family or for me to touch you. You cannot shake my hand." And then all our suspicions are confirmed. We know that the house is being bugged for sound and vision and that someone somewhere must have seen my shaking Ali and Reza's hands the day before. I know the dos and don'ts of Islam but Ali and Reza always struck me as pretty secular. The hidden watcher who reviews the footage from the house is clearly more hard-line.

Physical contact such as this is not viewed by Islam, particularly radical Islam, as a harmless transgression. The Hadith, the wider book of instructions as to how Muslims should live, states: *"It is better for you to be stabbed in the head with an iron needle than to touch the hand of a woman who is not permissible to you."* It goes on to explain that *"there is no doubt that for a man to touch a non-*mahram *(not permitted) woman is one of the causes of* fitnah *(turmoil, temptation), provocation of desire and committing* haraam *deeds."* This is, after all, revolutionary Iran, a country where adultery is punishable by death by stoning.

I can envisage the boot-faced clerics, choleric with rage, wagging their fingers, boiling over with their own piety, warning their people against an endless list of sins and temptations. You only need to turn on Iranian state TV to see such scenes played out, along with the periodic hangings and stoning of the transgressors. *Pour discourager les autres…*

Well, it's discouraged me all right. I will not shake Reza and Ali's hands again. But I won't have to obey the strictures of Islam much longer because we are to be freed this day.

"I understand completely," I tell them, keeping my distance.

"So what happens now?" I continue. "What is the plan for the day? When will we be freed?"

"Later, *Inshallah*."

Chapter Twenty Five: *Inshallah*

Inshallah – if God wills it. So deep does religious determinism run in the Islamic psyche that almost any sentence that involves the future is prefaced or epilogued with *Inshallah*. Back in Dubai, when I made arrangements with my Emirati, Egyptian or Lebanese friends to see them the next day or for our children to meet up at the weekend they would say: "Yes, 10 o'clock, on the beach, definitely! See you then, *Inshallah*." Or, my personal favourite, courtesy of a car-repair workshop in Al Quoz: "Yes, I have definitely fixed your car. The brakes are much better now. They will definitely work. *Inshallah*." Everything is caveated with reference to God's will.

The thing is, I'm not sure if God does want us freed. I'm not even sure He's noticed us.

When I first came to Dubai, I felt mildly amused, then as the months passed, mildly irritated by *Inshallah*. It was so often abused, so often used as a copout when promises were intended to be broken. Now every time it is said I want to scream. I go up to my room in search of silence. The word still races around in my head. There is one therapy that I have always known to work, one way to get the words out.

I pick up my Boggle notepad and my pen and I write this poem:

Home

Trapped in a prison of smiling faces,
Wearing a veil to hide my own,
Answering scores of repeated questions,
When will they let me go home?

Pouring with muck sweat under my burka,
My hopes depend on them,
Left alone for a million minutes,
Time stretches without end

Promises, promises roll from their lips,
But nothing is ever delivered.
Inshallah, say the smiling faces
But I think He's looking away

A birthday cake for a nightmare birthday
A puff and the candles are blown,
Oh please sign the papers in triplicate
And let me go back to my home.

Having written a poem I decide that I do not want it taken away from me. I wonder where I can hide it. I take the notepad and my sponge bag into the bathroom. I lock the door behind me and tear out the poem. I get a tampon, remove it from its cylindrical tube, wrap the poem round the tampon and reinsert it into its cylindrical case.

The day passes. We are like impatient children on a long car journey. *Are we there yet? Are we there yet? Are we free yet? Are we free yet?*

The answer is, that they will not free us. At least not this day. As the hours pass with agonising slowness, hope slowly dies. The bleakness of the despair that follows is the most God-awful feeling. It is like a sickness invading your soul, it leeches you of all energy. You have the feeling that you are falling, that you are breaking apart. We know that we cannot let despair take over, that we must fight it off but it is not easy to do. Brad begins to look very ill. I can feel a burning in my stomach: the acid of bitter disappointment. Rupert becomes scarily impassive. He is going into emotional lockdown mode. What do we do?

Rupert sees the way things are going. Diagnosing the dangers in plummeting morale he prescribes exercise. Brad declines to join us, which is probably just as well given his blood pressure.

Rupert and I go out into the hallway which forms a large square at the base of the stairs to the first floor and after a quick conference we drop down onto the tiled floor and start doing press ups.

We are something of exercise junkies in the first place and it has been very strange for us to be stuck almost unmoving, in one place for hours on end. Time to move! If we cannot move out of this house we can at least move within it. Our bodies long for movement so we will give it to them.

The Muscle come to watch. Inherently suspicious, they do not like any departure from the norm. Well tough, they can look away. They should do so anyway according to the strictures of Islam.

Exercising in a chador and a veil is weird. It seriously gets in the way. I think of the Nike ad with a woman powering along in a super sprint. *Just do it!* I superimpose a veil and a chador on her. *Not quite so easy to do it now is it, darling?* But it does the trick and it makes me smile. We flip over and do a series of sit-ups.

Next up, some aerobics. Up and down the stairs we go, me hooking up my chador so that I do not trip and go flying and end up flattening one of the Muscle who is watching us from the hallway. As we set off up the stairs again there is a brief discussion in Farsi behind us then I hear the sound of footsteps scurrying up the stairs after us. Clearly the Muscle has decided that we are up to something. At the top of the stairs we pause and then run down again passing Muscle One on the way. Muscle Two has evidently decided to stay downstairs. Perhaps he thinks we are the decoys and Brad is about to try and smash his way out. Or perhaps he's just lazy. But Muscle One continues to run up and down the stairs behind us in convoy like some kind of weird Islamic conga.

Muscle One gives up after several minutes realising, I suspect, that we are up to nothing more than just plain exercise. Rupert and I continue for about another ten minutes. Then we stand in the hallway, bracing our hands on our knees, feeling just a tiny bit pleased with ourselves.

One thing I have noticed is that in the context of powerlessness any tiny victories, any little acts of self-determination take on a massive and disproportionate importance. Whilst I believe in large part that things do happen for a reason, I do not subscribe to *Maktoob*. I do not believe that my fate is written. Much of my life has been spent carving my own destiny. One of the most difficult things about captivity is the impotence. You could just sit there and shrug and think *what can I do? There is nothing that I can do.*

But there is always something you can do, no matter how little. I have always loved the Dylan Thomas poem: *Do not go gentle into that good night, Rage, rage against the dying of the light.* I adapt it in my head: *Do not go passive into your captivity, Rage, rage against the casting of your fate.*

Rupert and I smile at each other. We are puffing and panting and sweating. And we have manufactured an excuse for a second shower.

After our shower (where as usual, we hold each other and whisper like lovers, all that we do not want picked up by the bugs), and after dinner, our Captors bring me my phone so that I can call my children. I have decided that I will not play by the rules anymore, that doing so has not secured our freedom. I have decided that we need a new approach. I have not told Rupert. I do not want him to try to stop me.

I feign a casual attitude as I tap out the phone number of our house in Dubai. My Captors have begun to give me more space as I make my call and they stand at the other side of the room. As usual, it takes me a good few minutes to get a connection. When I do, the nanny, Harriet picks up. She tells me that the children have gone to bed. I feel bitterly disappointed. But I have other things to do in this phone call and I need to get on with them. I have perhaps five seconds to play with. My heart begins to race. I blurt out: "We are being held against our will by the Iranians in Bandar Abbas. We do not have engine trouble, we have been kidnapped!"

Our Captors rush across the room screaming at me. They grab my phone, disconnecting the call.

"Why did you do that? You will be in trouble, you will be in such trouble!" They look panicked. They glance around the room as if there are unseen eyes watching us. Which of course, there are.

My husband and Brad look at me in horror.

"I said it because you are not letting us go free," I reply. I am relieved that they did not hit me, that they did not hurt me. I do not know what the consequences of my revelation will be. I hope that Harriet will tell our Embassy and Brad's, and that they will start exerting pressure on the Iranians to secure our release. What the consequences inside Iran will be, what the unseen watchers will do, I cannot tell.

"You should be patient," our Captors say, heatedly. "Patience got us nowhere," I reply.

Chapter Twenty Six: The Monster

The most immediate and visible consequence of my outburst is that for the next two days we are not allowed to talk to our children. There is no evidence that my declaration has had any positive effects. There are no visits from the British or the Australian Embassies, no suggestion that they are involved.

I can only hope that wheels are turning in the background. I find the lack of contact with my children, not being able to hear their voices, almost unbearable. To save my sanity, I have to shut down all feeling. I cannot allow myself to dwell on my children. Being apart from them causes me physical pain. The ache for them is like something I have never known. I have to try to dampen that down. I cannot not let my feelings surface. I fear that I will go mad if I do.

We are all on nodding terms with the monster in our head, with emotions that we do not let free, either for our own sake or for the sake of others. To function successfully as an adult we need to maintain self-control. I am also a control freak. I do not let go easily. But I am becoming aware that I need to act like the desperate mother that in reality I am. My self-control might be damaging our chances of freedom.

So I have to set the monster free. Half of me wants to anyway, the other half is terrified by the prospect. So, after yet another interrogation, after yet more hopes for release have been dashed, I begin to let go. I walk into the sitting room. Rupert looks up, comes to me, embraces me. "You all right?" he asks.

I hold him tight. I whisper into his ear. "Trust me." He stiffens slightly, clearly thinking *what the hell is she going to do now?* I pull back, giving him a look, trying to pour into that look the fact that I am all right, that I am in control, that I know what I'm doing. He watches me go. I head upstairs to our bedroom. Leaving the door partially open so that everyone can hear, I let the monster out.

I begin to cry. I begin to scream and wail. The sounds I make appal and horrify even me. I run around my room, I give vent to all the pain. Rupert comes up as I knew he would. He takes hold of my arm.

"They can't bear it downstairs," he says. He gives me a brief, complicit smile. He knows what I'm doing. "They say please can you stop."

Good! I thought to myself. Let them hear the consequences of what they are doing. Let them feel even a scintilla of my pain. Let them imagine how their wives would feel if they had been separated from their children. "I want my children!" I scream. "I want my children. I must see them. I cannot bear this anymore." And now the pain erupts, the monster is free, a kind of madness loosed. I let it rampage until all its emotions are spent.

Then, trembling, I sit on the edge of the bed. I feel hollowed out, empty. I do not feel myself. The myself I know has gone. I do not know the me it has left in its place. My eyes roam the room as if looking for somewhere to land, for something to grab onto. They alight on Boggle and my notepad. Acting like an automaton, I pick up pad and pen and I start to write.

Sanity

Sanity is a fragile thread,
Held at one end by the you you know
And at the other by the yous you don't.
How many of them are there
Deep in the folds of your mind?
Is it a democracy of competing voices, or does one shrilly silence them all?

And is that one the one you know,
Or a terrifying stranger?
Once you are silenced, will you ever find the old you
Or are you lost forever?

How do you shut them up, these others,

Put them back in their box?
You go back, if you can,
To the known and the normal.
If they release you.

Without reading the poem back to myself, I tear out the piece of paper and crumple it in my hand as if to throw it away. I go to the bathroom. I roll the paper and tuck it round another tampon. I do not splash cold water on my face. I do not want to make myself look better. I might not feel quite sure about who I am at that moment but I know what I have to do.

Our Captors get up as I walk in. They approach me. Their faces are creased in concern. "Are you all right?" They ask.

"Tomorrow it will be my son Tom's fifth birthday," I say, looking from one of them to the other. "We need to be there," I add, turning to glance at my husband.

"But if we cannot be there, please, please let us ring him."

"We will see what can be done," they reply.

Chapter Twenty Seven: Deliver Us From Evil

My husband can see the cost to me of my emotional outburst.

"Come on," he says to me. "We need to pray. Let's say the Lord's Prayer together." Rupert and I are not regular churchgoers, in fact we have not been to church at all in Dubai. However each of us does believe in God, in a power greater than ourselves. It takes the form of the Christian God but in essence it is God irrespective of how you paint him (or her). And, let's face it, we could do with a bit of celestial help.

But there is more to it than that. Rupert has long believed that ritual can be a sanity saver in its ability to reassure and to cement the concept of identity. In other words, to ground you. He would often tell me that in his Resistance to Interrogation course, the people who cracked first tended to be those who had no belief system outside of their own powers to fall back upon. I remember those conversations now.

Our days in this house have been punctuated by the regular, five daily calls to prayer which see our Captors and the Muscle regularly retreating to their prayer mats. Now it is our turn. Brad declines to join us. His passivity worries me. He has folded in upon himself.

So Rupert and I walk out into the hallway and we kneel down and together we start to say the Lord's Prayer. *Our father, which art in Heaven...* We can hear the Muscle approaching. I can sense their presence. *Hallowed be thy name...* I keep my eyes shut. This above all is something that they must be able to understand. *Thy kingdom come...* It is a prayer to God rather than to Allah and I don't know if this upsets them, but it is still a prayer. We are not heathens.

As we pray, I feel the rhythm and the melody of the words begin to soothe me. *For thine is the Kingdom...* The words take me back, many years and several thousand miles away, to a church in South Wales. *The power and the glory…* As he so often is, my husband is right. We repeat the prayer, over and over… *For ever and ever…*

The ritual as well and the words, as well as latent belief, all serve to restore me, to shore up my somewhat eviscerated sense of self… *Deliver us from evil…* I have always found those words to be the most powerful in the prayer. On this occasion, we have not seen evil. Not here. Not yet. That part of our misadventure is still to come.

Chapter Twenty Eight: Sleight of Hand

An hour later, Reza and Ali return with their twin briefcases. They unlock them, install the battery and hand over my phone. Now I have to ensure that all my emotions stay hidden, banked and under control so that I can talk to my children without upsetting them. I must be strong, a jolly, happy mother, frustrated at not being able to see them but nothing more. The prayer has helped me.

Harriet answers the phone. "Where are you?" she asks, urgently. My heart sinks. Did she not catch Bandar Abbas when I blurted it out two days ago? How can I tell her now? I cannot. At this moment, I must speak to my children.

"Please get the children," I implore her. I think she gathers from the tone of my voice not to ask more questions. I speak to all my children. I maintain to them the fiction that our boat has engine trouble. Still. I wish Tom a happy birthday for tomorrow, just in case I do not manage to speak to him on his big day. Five years old, my baby. And then I cannot speak any more. Wracked with silent sobs, I hand the phone to my husband. He talks to the children. He keeps himself together. He hangs up and hands the phone back to our Captors.

I have managed to regain my composure. I turn to them. "I didn't say all I wanted to say to Tom. Please can I ring him back?"

They are good men. They hand me back the phone. I tap out the numbers. The network is busy. And then, I have an idea. Whilst appearing to tap out the numbers, I send a text to Harriet. I have to type it out bit by bit, 13 characters at a time to match the tally of numbers that I have to dial to call home. I have to pause at regular intervals, complaining that the call has failed to go through, that the network is busy.

Finally I send it:

We are in Bandar Abbas being held by the Iranians.

I flick the phone to silent so that no tell-tale ping accompanies the sending of the text.

A text comes back immediately:

Who is this?

I think to myself *who the hell could it be? How many people do you know being held by the Iranians?*

I text back quickly:

Linda. Please alert the British Embassy.

And then I quickly tap out the number of the house again but as it is ringing I realise I have not deleted the texts. I cut off the call pretending that I did not get through again and I delete all the texts and then, taking the phone off silent, I ring home once more. I get through and I manage to talk to Tom, as normally as possible. I hang up. I hand back the phone. I smile.

Chapter Twenty Nine: Not Being There

Another day dawns. It is November 5th. My son Tom's fifth birthday. The Eid holiday is long since over. We cannot understand why we have not been freed. Why we are not all together, the five of us.

We were meant to be celebrating it in the Musandam Peninsula in Oman aboard a boat (yes, another boat) called the *Charlotte Rose*. This was an organised charter that would sail for two days and one night around the wonderful rugged coastline where we were going to search for turtles and dolphins, moor up off deserted beaches, light campfires and roast marshmallows under the stars. And celebrate Tom's fifth birthday. What is he thinking, my little boy? How can he rationalise both his parents abandoning him, not being there for his birthday…

How can I rationalise it? It is my fault that I am not there. However long and convoluted might be the chain of events that led to us being here, imprisoned in a box-like house with barred windows and locked doors on a naval compound, in a fundamental way I have let down my children. I should be there for them. With them. And I am not. And it cuts me up.

My husband, as always, has wise words. We sit next to each other on one of the single beds. He takes hold of my hands and looks me hard in the eye.

"We can't change what's happened. We can't go back." I see the pain in his face, but also determination, and resilience. "There's no point blaming yourself or me or Brad. That'll only bring you down. It is what it is."

Yeah, and what it is, is *crap*.

But I nod. He's right. Blame, recriminations, collapsing with grief will get us nowhere. My usual remedy for problems of any kind is action of some sort. Any sort, whether it is going for a run, phoning a friend, or working. Our options here are kind of limited. Limited but not non-existent.

At our morning conference in the shower, Rupert and I formulate a new plan.

After breakfast, our Captors arrive. We greet them with the usual pleasantries. I ask if I can speak to Tom, reminding them that today is his birthday. Reza and Ali are family men. They look in my eyes and they have some sense at least what I am feeling. Rupert masks his emotions. You cannot see anything through his eyes until those rare moments when he lets down his guard and the pain is all too visible. But only I see that in the quiet moments in our bedroom.

So I am allowed to ring Tom and wish him Happy Birthday. I apologise to him for not being with him. I maintain the fiction we still have engine trouble. And Tom with the magnanimity and selflessness that he seems to have had since birth says, "That's all right, Mummy. I know you would be here if you could. I do miss you though." At that point I have to fake a coughing fit and hand the phone to Rupert. I double up, grabbing my legs, sobbing silently.

After he has finished the call, Rupert tells me that Tom told him that Sarah Turner has organised a birthday party for him, that afternoon, with her own husband and three children who are matching ages and sexes to Hugh, Tom and Lara. For that as for many kindnesses, I shall be forever grateful to Sarah.

Chapter Thirty: Cry Havoc and Let Slip The Dogs Of War

After that phone call, whilst we still have my phone, Rupert asks for a favour.

"I am meant to be on a business trip the day after tomorrow," he explains to our Captors. That much is true. "My clients will think very badly of me if I fail to turn up. Could I ring our nanny so that she might pass on to my office a message re the meetings I have to cancel?"

Reza and Ali confer for a moment and then they nod. They hand him my phone. Rupert thanks them and dials a number. I sit on the sofa, affecting boredom, reading Alexander McCall Smith, again.

"Hello, Miss Harriet," he says loudly. "I cannot talk for long," he says, "but I need you to tell Robert Lawson, my PA, that I have to cancel the following four meetings. Please cancel Frank Gardner, Sir Peter De La Billière, Sheikh Khaled Al Sabah and Sir Graham Boyce." He frowns, says, "Damn, we were cut off. Oh well," he adds, "that was all I needed to say anyway." He hands the phone back to our Captors with a gracious smile of thanks.

I can visualise the person on the other end of the line hanging up. Robert Lawson, Rupert's PA, knew better than to speak when Rupert addressed him as Miss Harriet. He is smart, he is canny, he will know exactly what to do. I imagine him picking up his phone and saying in his soft Scottish burr:

"I am sorry to disturb you, Sir Peter, but I need to tell you some disturbing news. The Iranians are holding Rupert and Linda Wise captive in Bandar Abbas. (That bit I hope he will have learned from my text to our nanny.) They managed to get a message to me asking me to contact you. Please will you help…"

A line of Shakespeare from Julius Caesar pops into my head:
Cry havoc and let slip the dogs of war.

Frank, Sir Peter, Sheikh Khaled and Sir Graham are not Rupert's clients. They are very good, very old, and very useful friends. Frank Gardner is an eminent and renowned journalist. He is the security correspondent for the BBC. Just over a year earlier he was shot six times while on assignment in Riyadh by Al Qaeda terrorists. His cameraman was murdered. By a miracle, Frank survived though he was gravely injured and his legs have been left part paralysed by the bullets.

I will not say he is confined to a wheelchair because there is nothing confined about Frank. He is an amazing and inspiring man who regularly goes skiing, scuba-diving, and continues to report on security issues from various demanding locations around the world. (You can read his story in his powerful and wonderful book, *Blood and Sand.*)

We are sending a message to Frank not because we want media attention (we absolutely do not) but because Frank has access to several senior members of the UK government. He will be able to put pressure on them to secure our release, to ensure that everything that could be done is being done, whilst also ensuring a media blackout of our case. Frank and Rupert have been good friends for decades. They went to school together. Frank will be a powerful ally.

Peter de La Billière, or to give him his full title, General Sir Peter de La Billière, used to work with Rupert at Robert Fleming and Co Ltd, the merchant bank where Rupert worked for thirteen years. He is a good friend. He also happens to be the former commander of the SAS, the Special Air Service, Britain's elite special forces. Together he and Gen. Norman Schwarzkopf orchestrated Operation Desert Storm.

Sheikh Khaled Al Sabah hails from the Kuwaiti Royal family. He and Rupert have also known each other for decades. He is a very close friend of ours. He works for the Kuwait Investment Office. When Kuwait was invaded by Saddam Hussein he temporarily left his job to defend his homeland. With his family under a very real risk of execution, he managed to smuggle some of them out to Saudi Arabia, remaining behind with his aged uncle and aunt who refused to leave, concealing their identities with fake ID's. Their case was assisted, probably inadvertently, by the international media who made much of their belief that the entire Al Sabah family had fled the country. Khaled maintains that helped to save their lives. Khaled is big, powerful and carries himself like a warrior. There is a glint in his eyes that speaks of an ancient lineage of ruthless fighters. He is very much on the side of the angels and I'm glad to call him my friend.

Although I do not know Sir Graham Boyce well, I do know this much:

He is a distinguished former diplomat. He was the British ambassador to Qatar, Kuwait and to Egypt. His brother, Baron Boyce, was the first Sea Lord and later the Chief of the Defence Staff, the most powerful man in the British armed services.

We are putting our fate in the hands of these four ferociously capable, well-connected and powerful men. We feel more hopeful. And hope is everything.

Chapter Thirty One: SOS

Brad is not well. He is having trouble sleeping and his blood pressure is high. We are worried about him. We do not want to smoke in front of him in case we worsen his condition. Rupert has seen a door at the top of the stairs.

"Can we go onto the roof to smoke?" he asks. "We really do not want to make Brad sicker."

Reza and Ali confer. "Not during daylight hours," they say. "But at night, yes."

So that evening, Muscle One takes us up and escorts us out onto the roof. He then goes back inside and stays close but not so close as invade our privacy. (I have been listening to his footfalls.) Very decent of him.

November in the Middle East is the best time of year. The night is velvety dark. The stars above us are brilliant. The air is warm on our skin. After the chill of the air-conditioned house, being outside is blissful. We smoke and we talk, about the stars, about our children. We gaze up at the waxing moon. It gives me huge comfort, this moon. Far across the sea it will be shining down on our children. All our loved ones are under this same moon. We are not that far away after all…

We move around. There is a thick layer of dust on the roof. We drag our feet through it and we mark out in huge letters SOS.

If the British Embassy has managed to get one of the American satellites in position above Bandar Abbas then I'm hoping it will look down and that they will be able to locate the exact building that we are in. It's a long shot, but hey what we have to lose? It is another little victory, another little step away from *Maktoob* towards self-determination, towards freedom.

We light another cigarette, the nicotine flooding our veins like balm. That it might be poisoning us, sentencing us to cancer in years to come is irrelevant at that moment. *Whatever gets you through the night.* We grind out our stubs, go back down, rejoin Muscle One. He locks the door behind us and pockets the key.

Chapter Thirty Two: Prince of the Sea

Our Captors arrive the next morning as normal. But, in a departure from the most recent norm, Reza and Ali are all business: no smiles, no asking after our welfare. They bring with them two new faces. One military, one a civilian in a suit.

The military man has many coloured bars on the epaulettes of his immaculate dark navy uniform. He is medium height, very slim. He has an air of stillness about him but it is not an air of peace. It is an air of contained violence. He brings to mind a cobra: sleek, dark and powerful, wholly aware of its own lethal potential, poised and ready to strike. He has eyes that are hard, resilient, and a touch jaded, as if he has seen it all. As if he will see it all, one way or another. The other thing that strikes me immediately is his burning intelligence.

He nods at us in greeting. We nod back in silence. I can feel in the air that Rupert sees in this man what I see: a whole new level of threat.

Our Captors talk to this new man in Farsi. I do not speak the language but I recognise the bit of Arabic that punctuates their address: *Amiral*. The condensed version of *Amir al Bahar*, meaning 'Prince of the Sea.'

This man has an air of regal command about him. He wears it lightly, there is no bombast or bluster to him, but the power he wields is evident from the cringing of the Muscle and the explicit deference of our Captors.

"The Admiral has flown down from Teheran to talk to you," they say portentously. I feel a flush of fear. The big guns have arrived.

Chapter Thirty Three: Know Thine Enemy

The Admiral and the civilian interrogate my husband first. I watch them walk off. I see to my surprise that the Admiral has a pronounced limp. I wonder when he got it. Some kind of war wound no doubt. I think of the conflicts he might have fought in. I reckon he is in his early fifties. That would have put him in his mid to late 20s during the Iran Iraq war of 1982 to 1988. I think about that war. I try and remember what I know of it. Know thine enemy.

Allow me to digress here, because the scale of this war, and what it represented, left and leaves an indelible mark on the Iranian psyche and also explains their ongoing paranoia.

After the Shia revolution in Iran in 1979, neighbouring Iraq, Sunni-controlled but home to a majority Shia population comprising 55% to 60% of the total, felt particularly threatened. Also threatened were Bahrain with a large Shia population and, crucially, the Eastern Province of Saudi Arabia (where 60% of the population is Shia) and where 25% of the world's oil reserves are found. The Eastern Province is the key, swing producer within Opec and as such is responsible for controlling/ maintaining global oil prices.

The oil producing countries of the Gulf, along with the US, UK and the West in general, feared the formation of a Shia Crescent in the Persian Gulf that would destabilise the region and threaten to disrupt global oil supplies and prices.

It became politically expedient for the West to back Saddam Hussein. Saddam, essentially a secular leader, was notionally a Sunni Muslim, and as such could be used by the West as a regional bulwark against revolutionary Shiism.

Emboldened by this support, and operating on the belief that the Iranian armed forces were massively weakened by the removal of their officer class (executed by Revolutionaries as part of their purge of the Shah's ruling elite), Saddam Hussein invaded Iran in 1982.

The Iranians found themselves defending their Revolution, their religion, and their Homeland. They lost over one million soldiers, a casualty rate which was roughly equivalent to ours in The First World War. As the Iran Iraq war went on, year after year, Iran conscripted ever younger men, ultimately sending into battle boys in their late teens wearing around their necks plastic keys blessed by Mullahs – the keys to Paradise.

The strength of the Iranian resolve and their resilience surprised the Iraqis, who found themselves in danger of losing this war.(Saddam had ignored one of the fundamental lessons of history – never attack a revolution.) But Saddam had powerful allies. The West and much of Arabia were happy to step in and help fight the war against what they regarded as a significant threat. The Western allies might not particularly have liked Saddam Hussein, but that didn't alter the realpolitik. As the Americans said at the time: *"He might be a sonofabitch but he's our sonofabitch."*

The United States was involved in several missions against Iran directly, Operation Praying Mantis and Operation Prime Chance to name but two, but it also supplied considerable help on the logistical and material front to Iraq, sending in massive quantities of resupply via Kuwait and Jordan.

Finally in 1988 a ceasefire was negotiated. Neither side could be said to have emerged victorious. But one thing was clear. The world was ready to stand against Iran. Before the deposition of the Shah and the revolution, Iran and the West had been allies. When the Iranians took over the US embassy in Teheran in 1979 (the siege lasted for 444 days), they declared their own enmity towards the Great Satan and the West as a whole, but with the West's backing of Saddam Hussein and with the US's active prosecution of the war against Iran, the level of enmity between Iran and the rest of the world rose to new and even more dangerous levels.

It is against this backdrop that the paranoia of the Iranian state and its extreme vigilance against the incursions of hostile agents needs to be understood.

After several hours, Rupert emerges. I can see from his eyes how tired he is. This interrogation is far more demanding than those that have gone before. And now it's my turn.

I am called in to the interrogation room by the civilian man. He is colourless and nondescript in his grey suit. He is one of those people that seem to be attempting to make themselves as inconspicuous as possible.

I take my usual seat. The questioning begins. The civilian is there in the role of interpreter. The Admiral would appear not to speak English. He asks his questions in a quiet, melodious, well-modulated voice. He looks at me as he asks the questions, keeping his eyes on me as the translator relays them in English.

It seems obvious to me that the Admiral is battle hardened and acutely aware. I do not think that the dumb blonde routine will work with him. I shall have to try another tack. I will have to appeal to his intelligence.

The Admiral's questions are roughly the same as those of Ali and Reza, but he focuses more on the various aspects of our boat and on Brad's proficiency as a captain. He asks me lots of questions about Brad, which I really can't answer. I have to explain that I don't really know that much about Brad. I wonder why he is so interested in him. The man is patently not a spy.

After he has been interrogating me for several hours, I play my wild card. I look at the Admiral directly, I do not look at the translator. And I say to him, "Interrogate me for as long as you like. Keep me awake for days on end, ask me any question you want to. And then form an opinion as to my intelligence. Do you honestly think that I would allow my husband to bring me on a spying mission where in any event, I would see less from the deck of my boat than any satellite could see via look down. I have three young children at home. Do you really believe I would risk not seeing them grow up for such paltry intelligence? And if I were a spy, do you think that the British intelligence agencies would risk me on such an asinine mission or that I would allow them to?" I pause. "If after interrogating me for all that time, you still think that I'm a spy, then hold me and keep me. But if you think I'm not, then you must let me and my husband and Brad go free."

I am shaking. I have thrown down the gauntlet. I have offered to deal. This is a pledge that I would honour. I can only hope that he might be moved to honour it too.

As I speak I see his eyes widen in surprise. Then I see a faint smile flicker across his features. I have made contact. He understands me all right. Then the moment is broken and he looks away from me and speaks to the interpreter, still maintaining the pretence that he cannot understand English. The interpreter translates:

"The Admiral says that is enough for now. He will talk to you later."

I smile, I nod, I get up and walk from the room. My skin is tingling, I feel electric. I have played my card.

Chapter Thirty Four: The Test

We have lunch and then the Admiral interrogates Brad. After several hours, he emerges with Brad and calls for us all to congregate in the sitting room. Reza and Ali join us. The Muscle hover officiously nearby. But there is no sign of the interpreter.

The Admiral produces a book. It would appear to be some sort of international yachtsman's handbook. Abandoning all pretence, the Admiral then proceeds to quiz us in fluent English on the finer points of sailing. He speaks with a faint US accent.

"What colour lights should be lit when coming into or going out of port?" he asks us. That and a score of other questions.

He quite clearly knows his stuff. Rupert and I know very little. That does not seem to bother the Admiral. We never pretended to be sailors, just hapless tourists.

The Admiral turns to Brad and proceeds to interrogate him: *What passages has he sailed? What races has he completed? What kind of boats has he crewed?*

Brad answers these questions easily enough. He is a seasoned sailor. He has taken part in the Sydney to Hobart race multiple times. He has crossed the Atlantic several times. He is a professional sailor, has been for over twenty-five years.

The Admiral listens to this slouched back in his chair with a dismissive and faintly disbelieving mien. He then proceeds to grill Brad on some of the more technical aspects and rules of sailing.

Whether it is through exhaustion, nervousness or perhaps a lack of theoretical knowledge, Brad answers quite a few of the questions incorrectly.

This enrages the Admiral. He gives Brad a very hard time. He does not conceal his contempt for the captain for failing this test that he has set him.

After the Admiral has gone, Brad really looks ill. This is terrible for his blood pressure. But there is no rest for Brad, or for Rupert and myself. We hear voices at the door. Other men have arrived to interrogate us.

Chapter Thirty Five: Multiple Ministries

Whether it is a result of the British Embassy contacting the Iranian Government, or whether it would have happened anyway, we three hostages now seem to have come onto the radar of a vast and bewildering array of Iranian Ministries.

Over the next few days we are interrogated by so many people that I lose count. We are questioned morning, noon and night. I speak so much that my veil becomes damp and sticks to my mouth. But at least I can use my eyes to signal the truth I speak. At least I do not have to cover my entire face in one of those bird-like contraptions with a nose beak or wear one of those all-encompassing blue robes that hangs from the head down to the ground and seems beloved of the Taliban for their womenfolk. The Burqa.

It strikes the irreverent part of me that peels off in my head and watches proceedings from an ironic distance that I have spoken this intensively, repeatedly answering the same questions with just a few twists here or there, on several occasions before in my life. Doing book tours in the United States:

Good morning, it's the New York Times… Welcome to NBC and Today with Maria Shriver… Hi, this is Katie Couric on Good Morning America… Good afternoon, it's the Wall Street Journal. Goodday, it's Fortune Magazine. Hi there, it's Glamour Magazine. Greetings, it's Vanity Fair. Then I was trying to sell books. Now I am trying to avoid prison.

Rupert is also interrogated exhaustively by first an incompetent Arabic speaker and secondly by a highly competent one. Whether this is a final box to be ticked before we are freed or whether it is a whole new avenue that takes us deeper into the Iranian machine, we do not know. After each one of these interrogations, forms in Farsi are produced. We stick to our method of writing out our set piece in English attesting to the truth of our answers and then signing our names.

This might all sound quite bureaucratic but the fear is always there. Any one of these interrogations could lead to us being charged, being sentenced, being dispatched to a real prison.

When we aren't being interrogated we all fall prey to dark thoughts. I think about my children, wondering how they are. I ask myself: How long can I stand to be separated from them? How much of this can I bear? Two weeks? One month? Six months? A year? How did Amanda Lindhout, Terry Waite, Brian Keenan and John McCarthy and all the long-term hostages manage it? How did they stay sane when they were beaten and tortured and held in appalling conditions?

We have no idea if we will still be here in a week, in a month, in six months, in a year.

Perhaps here I should tell you of the fate of the close friend of one of Rupert's relations (See Appendix Two). Roger Cooper is a friend of Rupert's swashbuckling brother-in-law, Doug Barker. Doug, now dead, was a bilingual Russian-speaking businessman who among other things was a member of the Joint Services Interrogation Wing. Doug's friend Roger was arrested by the Iranians in the 1980's. Found guilty of spying, he was given the following sentence: ten years in prison followed by execution. Can you imagine that? Living every single minute of every single hour of every single day for ten years, knowing all the while that at the end of it you would be taken out into some dusty yard and shot. Or hanged.

Fortunately, after a rapprochement between the UK and Iran (temporary!) Roger Cooper was freed after five years. After his release he noted drily with possibly a touch of English understatement that "anyone who has been to a British boarding school is well able to handle an Iranian prison."

We do not know if ten years plus execution will be our fate. Or five years followed by release. It might just be five more days… The uncertainty is what does my head in. The idea of not being there to watch my children grow up, not being a mother to them, is almost unbearable.

Most of the time we are too tired and too disheartened to do our crazy exercises. We are no longer allowed to go up on the roof for a cigarette and a breath of fresh air. Perhaps our SOS in the dust has been spotted…

What we do do every night is collapse in front of the television to watch, again, *The Last Samurai* or *Die Hard*, our other favourite. (Am I beginning to live Groundhog Day?) As *Die Hard* plays out with its crashes bangs and wallops, I find myself listening out for those same sounds in stereo, coming from outside our house. While Bruce Willis fights the bad guys on screen in front of me, are the SAS outside, black clad, incapacitating the guards, getting ready to blow a hole through the wall? Half of me is prepared for a flash bang to come smashing through the window. I am ready to hurl myself to the ground and take cover under the table. I know it is incredibly unlikely that the SAS will come storming in. The political and logistical complexities involved in infiltrating Iran and then exfiltrating us from the midst of a naval base would be a challenge even for them. But I'm still ready.

Chapter Thirty Six: A Bargain and a Warning

The SAS do not come. But there is action of a different sort. After yet more interrogations with yet more ministries, we are told to pack our bags.

"What's happening? Where are we going?" I ask. The Admiral takes me aside.

"You are going to be taken to meet members of your Embassy. I hope that you will then be freed. You have been lucky so far."

"What do you mean?"

"Well, you have been interrogated by teams from the Judiciary in Bandar Abbas, Naval Intelligence from Teheran, the Ministry of the Interior from Teheran and the Ministry of Foreign Affairs from Teheran. Pretty much the only relevant entity that has not interrogated you has been the Revolutionary Guard. Things would be very different if you had been. Luckily for you, they would not appear to know of your existence yet." His face is grave.

The word *yet* hovers in the air. I have a sense that time is running out. This is the first occasion that I have been made aware of the competing and often antagonistic factions within the Iranian regime. On one side is the visible apparatus, on the other is the shadowy world of the Revolutionary Guard. They are the teeth arm of the Revolution. The extremist Islamists and the hard men who hide behind the ranting clerics and their cloaks of religiosity.

It is to fund the Revolutionary Guard and their hold on the power, and their weapons programs and their overseas terrorist forays (supporting Assad in Syria, Hamas in the Palestinian territories and Hezbollah in Lebanon) and their more general attempts to enlarge the Shia crescent, that a significant proportion of Iran's oil revenues are diverted (as well as huge payoffs from allowing in heroin from across the border with Afghanistan).

Heroin addiction is a huge problem inside Iran and pays well, like everywhere else. They are also funded by revenues from the Bonyads, the holding companies of the assets confiscated from the Shah and the pre-Revolution elite. The Bonyads have huge portfolios of real estate, factories, mines, farms as well as financial assets.

If any of Iran can be said to be the Evil Empire, it is the Revolutionary Guard.

I digest this stroke of candour.

The Admiral strokes his chin, thoughtful. He hasn't finished yet. "Of course, you were lucky to have got that far…" Again I ask what he means.

"If you had sailed in a few hours later, after darkness had fallen, then no questions would have been asked. You and your boat would have been shot straight out of the water."

I lower my head. I park this away somewhere deep. It is too big to process.

I look up again, meet his gaze. "Thank you," I say quietly, "for your help."

The Admiral has been instrumental in moving this on. It is obvious from the behaviour of all those around him that he is by far the most high-ranking person in our midst. (It is evident too that he has a profound love for this complicated country of his.)

But I cannot be effusive in my thanks to this man for fear that it would backfire on him. I've learned my lesson after shaking hands with Reza and Ali and being aware that they were then heavily reprimanded for it.

I ask the Admiral where he learned his English and he smiles at me. He knew that I knew that he could speak English from the outset.

"I went to College in the United States," he says. He takes a moment. I can see the memories of another life scrolling through his mind.

"You know what they thought you had done," he adds, coming back to the here and now. I shake my head.

"There was a bomb that went off on our border with Iraq. We have not yet found the bombers. We are under considerable pressure to come up with the culprits. It was suggested that it might be you." His conversational tone belies the grimness of his eyes.

I think of Roger Cooper and his ten years followed by execution. I think of the paranoia of the state and its tendency to see evil and threat all around. Especially if you are the wrong nationality.

"Yes, that's likely," I say.

He laughs. In a country where the currency of the accused is denial, for good reason, my response amuses him. "I told them that you were not a bomber. I added that your husband was not a bomber either. And neither was your Captain," he adds, lip curling.

It's funny, this man possibly because he has been educated in the United States, seems to accept the theoretical possibility that I might have been a bomber, not just the wife of a bomber. It is evident to me that it had not occurred to any of the other interrogators that I might have been a bomber. I thank God for this chauvinism because if I am not a bomber (or a spy) and if I am not a dupe who has gone along to deflect attention from a 'mission', then my husband is not a bomber (or a spy) either, and we can go free… Rather than hang.

We say a formal Goodbye. I watch the Admiral limp away. I remember the gauntlet I had thrown down to him: *interrogate me, assess my intelligence, then tell me if you think I am a spy. If you do, then charge me, if you do not then set me free.* It is obvious that he intends to honour the bargain.

However, we have had our hopes raised, only to see them dashed so often in the past days that although I am delighted that finally we will be meeting members of our Embassy, I refuse to let my spirits soar. I will only believe that I'm free when I am in an aircraft exiting Iranian airspace.

Chapter Thirty Seven: The Execution Chamber

Rupert and I and Brad, with our paltry belongings, leave behind the house that has been our prison for ten days. For the first time in what seems like ages, I feel the sun on my face. To be outside, to see the colours, to feel the air against my skin, or what little skin I am permitted to expose, is a momentary bliss. But there is no time to linger. With a sense of nervous urgency, Reza and Ali usher us into a waiting minibus. Soon we are out into the traffic of Bandar Abbas.

My heart is pounding. Where are we going? We drive at breakneck speed through the city, accelerating past the lumberingly graceful old American cars, turning off the main thoroughfare into a warren of narrow streets lined with vendors selling huge watermelons and mothers in good 'hijab' walking their children to school. We leave the bustling centre and drive into what appears to be a wasteland of deserted, rundown, unoccupied buildings. Mangy dogs roam for scraps. This is not good. I cannot see how any members of our Embassy would be based in such a place.

The driver parks in an underground car park. It is empty. This looks like something out of a movie that ends badly. The driver turns to us, tells us to get out of the minibus. Tells us to walk through the car park towards the stairwell. Tells us to go up the stairs. He follows us. Who is he? I wonder. He is wearing the Shalwar Kameez style of dress. He is Iranian, but he does not seem to be linked to Ali or Reza in any way. They follow some steps behind him. They appear extremely uneasy.

The tension in the air is electric. I am half expecting to be shot in the back. I know that Rupert and Brad fear the same thing. It's obvious from their body language and from the fear that hovers, rank in the air. We are taken into a room. The floors and the walls are bare concrete. There is no glass in the large windows. It is probably 30 feet up. Will we be pushed out? Would it classify as defenestration if there is no glass, wonders my irreverent part. There are two people waiting in the room: a man, British-looking, wearing a suit and a woman, Iranian-looking, her hair covered but her face visible, the rest of her body swathed by her Chador. They do not look like assassins. They are smiling at us. They walk forward, hands extended. "Hello," they say. "We are from the British Embassy. Welcome."

Chapter Thirty Eight: Bravery

I don't think I have ever been so delighted to meet anyone in my life. I will not go into detail about these representatives of the British Embassy who we are lucky enough to meet, save to say that they are immensely brave. The woman is Iranian. Working for the British puts her in a very exposed position. She was and is one of the bravest women I have ever met.

She takes me into her arms and gives me a bear hug. I cannot tell you how much that means, how great is the comfort in that simple gesture.

"So, you three have had a bit of an eventful time," says the man.

"A bit of an ordeal," says the woman with a smile full of compassion and understanding.

"Tell us a bit about what's been happening," says the man.

For the next half an hour or so, we quickly fill them in. We cannot talk entirely freely, as Reza and Ali are with us. The driver hovers in the doorway. We have no secrets to hide but we need to be careful and delicate. We skip over some of the idiocies of our detainment, like the Boggle incident. We gratefully acknowledge how well Reza and Ali have treated us.

We are dying to ask questions about the other side, about how the Embassy has been dealing with our kidnapping, about what has been told to our children, but this is not territory that we can explore with Reza and Ali and the mysterious driver present. It is evident too from the high speed, evasive driving that brought us to this out-of-the-way and improbable location that we are being hidden, that some agency very much not on our side might be looking for us, that we are by no means out of danger yet, so we say nothing, we ask nothing save *what is the plan?*

Chapter Thirty Nine: The Hormuz Hotel

The plan is that we keep moving. After some discussion between Reza and Ali and the representatives of the British Embassy, it is agreed that we will be taken to a hotel where we will spend the afternoon and the night before leaving the next morning for the airport in Bandar Abbas from whence we will take a flight to one of the outlying islands that has direct flights on to Dubai.

Sounds a wonderful plan to us. But at the moment it remains a plan. I cannot allow my hopes to rise. We are driven off. More of the high speed, evasive stuff.

After about twenty minutes we arrive at the hotel. It is of the most brutal dictator-chic Eastern European design that has found a spiritual home in various locations around the Middle East; a flat fronted concrete structure with a large nationalistic emblem decorating the very top of it.

I love it! It is not an Iranian naval base. There are no secured perimeter walls surrounding us, no gatehouses with armed guards. I am aware however of shadows that materialise in the foyer and follow us at a discreet distance as the British Embassy officials show us to our rooms.

"We have neighbouring rooms down the hallway," they say. "Please do not leave your rooms," they add with apologetic smiles. "We'll come and get you if you'd like to join us downstairs for dinner."

Brad says he'll see how he feels later. Rupert and I nod enthusiastically. We've seen far too much of four enclosing walls to wish to stay inside our room any longer than necessary. Besides, I reckon we would be safer in a public place. The sense of threat still hovers in the air. We can see it in the extreme nervousness of Reza and Ali which is mirrored in a more controlled stiff upper lip way by the British Embassy man. The Iranian woman, I shall call her Nasrin, is unflappably cool and collected though, smiling and charming as if this were no more than a delightful social occasion.

"Seven thirty?" she asks.

"Thank you, yes, seven thirty is good for us." Nothing else in our busy schedule. We close the door. I pull off my chador and my veil, drop them on the floor, overjoyed to be rid of them, if only for a while.

Rupert and I pad around our small room. It is clean, it is functional. It is also almost certainly bugged. Out comes Boggle.

After playing maybe ten games, my curiosity gets the better of me and I open the door just to see if it is locked from the outside. It is not locked but I see looking at me with interest an Iranian man in Shalwar Kameez loitering perhaps fifteen feet away down the corridor. I look at him, he looks at me and we understand each other perfectly. I close the door again and lock it from the inside. What I don't know is which side he is on. Does he work for the British Embassy or is he from one of the shadowy Iranian Ministries?

Following a practice that I have long since adhered to when staying in questionable hotels in dodgy parts of the world, I pull up a chair and wedge it under the door handle.

Rupert and I resume Boggle. We are pretty equally matched. We reckon that if a world championship were called right now, we would have a very good chance of winning.

I dress for dinner. This comprises putting on my chador and my veil and adjusting them to ensure my modesty. The First Secretary and Nasrin knock on our door at exactly seven thirty. We head out into the hallway. The shadow is still there. He joins us in the lift. We nod to him. *Let's keep this civilised.*

Rupert and I sit with the two representatives of the British Embassy. Brad stays in his bedroom. He is feeling unwell. Four shadows flank us at two neighbouring tables. We do not ask who they are, on whose side they might be. We do not talk of freedom, we do not talk of our hopes. We stick to innocuous subjects, but it is wonderful just to sit with the illusion at least of liberty and to talk with these people who are a link with our homeland, who are unequivocally on our side.

Chapter Forty: The Worst Day

The next day is possibly the worst day of my life. I suspect the same holds true for Rupert and Brad.

It begins well enough. The First Secretary and Nasrin come knocking at our door at seven in the morning. We are dressed and ready, packed and waiting. We pick up Brad and tailed by a shadow we go down in the lift.

"Do you mind if we skip breakfast?" asks the First Secretary. "We'd like to get you on your way to the airport." We shake our heads. We don't mind at all. We hurry out through Reception into a waiting minivan with a driver at the wheel. There seems to be a bit of a commotion going on outside but the shadow slams the door on us and we speed off so we can't really see what's going on. We arrive at the teeming airport. On the forecourt it is a typical third world maelstrom of suitcases, shouting, barging and emotion.

We are hurried inside. At the security check Rupert and Brad are taken off to be patted down by a man while I am searched by a very angry woman. She mutters and wags her finger at my dress which ends about three inches above my ankles. She yanks it down but it is lycra and so it just bounces back up. Furious, she pulls from a drawer a pair of black knee-length tights and orders me to put them on. Not a good look with flip flops, I am tempted to tell her. I balance on one foot at a time and pull them on. Now respectably dressed I pass through security. Rupert and Brad also have a hard time because they are wearing shorts. Understandably, they did not pack trousers for a two-day voyage.

The air-conditioned terminal is crowded, we attract a lot of attention, probably because of the way we are dressed and the fact that we are so obviously Westerners and that we have with us an entourage of Westerners and Iranians. Rupert, Brad and I sit on a crowded bench with Reza and Ali.

Nasrin and the First Secretary are rushing to and fro from one ticket desk to another. They are trying to get us tickets for the flight to Kish Island and then on to Dubai. They appear to be having some problems. They are becoming increasingly anxious. Reza and Ali keep glancing around nervously. They are more than worried, they are frightened. We are too. My body feels as if it is vibrating with tension. Brad looks ill again. His colour is high. His blood pressure is rocketing. Rupert and I both normally have low blood pressure but I'm sure ours is rising high. My husband is trying to stay calm but I can feel the tension pumping off him in waves.

Nasrin returns, face grave.

"We are having trouble getting your tickets," she says. "All the flights are full."

I have the horrible sensation that time is running out. Being so near to freedom and yet seemingly being thwarted by something as prosaic as a full flight is almost unbearable. We move on to a gated area, presumably in the hope that we might get some waitlisted seats. We wait and we wait. Other passengers look at us with open hostility. Why? Are we so obviously their enemies? We continue to wait for several hours in this almost unendurable limbo.

And then the situation takes a turn very much for the worse.

Chapter Forty One: The Thug

Six large, burly, hard faced men in civilian suits approach the gate at speed. They do not look like passengers. They look like thugs. "Secret police," whispers Nasrin. She straightens up as if ready for battle.

Reza and Ali look like rabbits in the headlights. They are almost frozen with fear. The First Secretary moves in front of us. We of course hope that it is somebody else in the queue they are interested in but inevitably it is us. The thugs stop feet away, glowering at me and Rupert and Brad. They turn to the Iranians and to the First Secretary and they begin to shout. A loud and angry discussion proceeds in Farsi between them and our Embassy officials. Reza and Ali are ordered to leave. Whoever these thugs are, they outrank our naval officers in sheer power and it is obvious that any form of resistance is out of the question. Reza and Ali give us looks of abject apology.

"I'm sorry," they each say. "We must leave you. We will pray for you and for your children." I know they will too.

I feel the tears burning my eyes but I will not cry in front of the thugs.

Reza and Ali walk away. I know that I will never see them again. It has been strange this friendship that has developed between us and our erstwhile Captors. Stockholm syndrome but not quite. They did not convert me to a cause. Instead we found a common cause: our humanity.

They had become friends. It is obvious that these new men are enemies.

The First Secretary and Nasrin are protesting loudly at something that we do not understand. Back and forth goes the argument with neither side yielding. The three of us watch. I feel sick to my stomach. And then, the discussion turns violent.

I have seen evil a few times in my life and the chief of these six men is without any doubt, evil. Thickset with a snub nose and small, hard eyes, I shall name him the Thug. He takes both his hands and shoves the First Secretary hard in the chest, sending him sprawling. Then he spins round and moves towards us. The Embassy man bravely comes back and tries to interpose his body between us and them. The Thug punches him in the chest and face and stomach. The airport security police run up, weapons at the ready.

We are outnumbered, we are outgunned and we are once more in enemy hands.

Chapter Forty Two: The Plan

International law has no remit in Iran. We forget that at our peril.

"I'm so sorry," says the First Secretary. "There is a change of plan. These men have come down from Teheran. They are insisting that we release you to them so that they might take you there for further interrogation."

It is the first time that I have seen Nasrin's composure falter.

"We are truly sorry," she says. "This is outrageous behaviour and we shall protest it most strongly, but there is nothing we can do."

We look around at the armed men. There is truly nothing that they or we can do, save say goodbye. One of the thugs grabs the First Secretary and manhandles him away.

"I will ensure that the British Ambassador, Richard Dalton, is waiting for you in Teheran," he shouts as he is dragged off. "He will intercept you. He will stop this."

We can only pray this will happen. The plan is in tatters. Another thug grabs Rupert by the arm. I pray that my husband's self-control does not fail him now. I know exactly what he wants to do, what his instinct primes him to do. He wants to take an almighty swing at this bastard and knock him flying. He wants to keep punching him until he goes down and stays down. But he does not do this. Training and discipline and self-control take over and he allows himself to be dragged along. What choice does he have? I think this thug would love nothing more than for Rupert to resist arrest. It would then give him the excuse the look in his eyes suggest he really, badly wants: to beat Rupert senseless, to probably beat the rest of us senseless too. Deprived of that, he just yanks Rupert forward, parting the crowds like a daemonic Moses.

Another thug grabs Brad while the two other henchmen follow behind.

Mercifully, I am thug-free. One of the more beneficial strictures of Islam is that they are not allowed to touch me. At least in public. I suspect that in private there is very little that these men would not do.

We are taken to a cafe. Brad, Rupert and I sit with our new Captors. I wonder who these men are. Are they Revolutionary Guard? I pray that they are not. We chain smoke. I do not cry. I do not shout. I do not look at our new Captors. I've gone into shutdown mode though: inside, my whole body feels hollowed out with despair, and with fear. This is a new low. To have been so close to escape and then to have been rearrested is the cruellest blow. We are not offered food or water, but none of us could eat anyway.

Chapter Forty Three: Evasion

We are escorted on board a plane. Rupert, Brad and I sit in one row, flanked fore and aft by a row of thugs. The flight is full. They obviously had no problem in persuading nine would-be travellers to give up their seats.

I wonder if there is anything we can do at this stage. I look around at our fellow passengers. They studiously avoid catching my eye. They can see the power of these men. That they do not want to cross them is evident. There is no help on board this plane.

After a while I turn and glance at one of the thugs.

"I need to go to the loo," I say. He looks blank. "Toilet!" I mouth. I do need to go but I also want to see if I get any inspiration on the way. He nods. He follows me as I walk along the aisle. I feel the eyes of everyone on the plane glance my way. I go in, lock the door behind me. I come out a few minutes later and immediately he pushes in past me. I can hear him rummaging about, evidently examining the loo in forensic detail to see if I have secreted any notes or letters or anything else that might be perceived as contraband inside. I have not.

I go back to my seat and I close my eyes and I try and shut out all thought. We land at an airport. There is no 'welcome to Teheran and thanks for flying with us' spiel, either in English or in Farsi. The sky is grey. It is overcast. The plane taxis to a halt. Our captors unbuckle and get up and gesture to us to do the same. A mobile staircase is being pushed towards the plane. Will the British Ambassador be there, waiting for us? We hope, we pray desperately that he will be.

But he is not. Instead, waiting for us is a minivan with blacked out windows. We are pushed into it, the door slams and the van roars off at speed through a side gate. Then the man at the wheel proceeds to engage in high-speed evasive driving which makes our earlier experiences in Bandar Abbas look tame.

Abruptly, we screech to a halt. Doors open and we are pulled out onto the hard shoulder of a chaotic and fast moving highway. Traffic screams by perilously close. There is an overpass with cars hurtling by above us. We are manhandled into a different minibus which is waiting for us, engine idling. Doors slam before we are in our seats and it screeches off into the falling night. Obviously this manoeuvre is designed to lose any pursuers such as the British Ambassador if he has managed to get on our tail. Where are they taking us?

We drive on. After about ten minutes, the rattling of the minibus has opened up a small gap between the curtain and the edge of the window. I angle my head surreptitiously and manage to peer out. It has started to snow! I see a blur of big, feathery snowflakes, speeding traffic and dingy buildings. I see high walls topped with razor wire. They go on for a very long way. Is this a prison? The notorious Evin where foreigners are held, where the worst of Iran's real or perceived criminals are interned prior to execution? Is this our destination? I try to open the curtain some more. One of the thugs spots me and slaps my hand. So much for not touching me. He yanks the curtain fully shut.

Chapter Forty Four: Teheran

It seems another world after the golds and blues and balmy warmth of the Persian Gulf. My glimpses suggest a dystopian nightmare of a city. I am being wildly unfair. It might be beautiful and wonderful. But not here, not now, not to me.

Teheran. Even the word sounds like a mispronunciation of *Terror.* What do I know of it? It covers a larger area than London and has a bigger population. It is bedevilled by smog. Its nuclear scientists have a habit of dying in car bombs, or at the end of a bullet fired by an Israeli assassin riding pillion on a high-powered motorbike, faster than the maximum 125ccs allowed by the state in their attempts to hinder such assassinations. It nestles in the foothills of the Elburz Mountains which rise to nearly 19,000 feet. It is an earthquake zone. If we are not killed by this kamikaze driving, then maybe an earthquake will get us. It was home to the siege of the US Embassy which lasted for 444 days. I remember the TV images of rioting mobs overrunning the Embassy compound. (More recently we have seen Iranian pitted against Iranian as protesters against the regime are brutally beaten down by the *Basij*, the Islamist thugs employed by the Revolutionary Guard. We also see images of centrifuges, of buildings in the desert underneath which are said to lie the vast uranium processing plants.) Cheery place.

We drive on. I can only hope that we are now far beyond the razor-wired walls. I'm desperate to know where we're going. After a few minutes, I manage to ease the curtain open again a couple of inches. The snow-covered tarmac on the side of the road reflects the sickly orange lamplight. The buildings are less dingy. We are passing high rises, apartment blocks and office buildings. We would appear to be in central Teheran.

And then we pull up. Outside what looks like a hotel. I sit back blinking in surprise. We are told to get out of the van. "Do not speak!" Thug Number One hisses at us. He walks so close to me I can feel the air of controlled violence he is suppressing. I can smell the synthetic and animal tang of his sweaty suit. We are escorted into the hotel foyer.

I look around wildly. I see large signs saying in English *Welcome to the 2005 Annual International Mining Conference.* Normal life plays on around our nightmare. This is surreal. The foyer is thronging with delegates of a vast range of nationalities. There must be Brits and Americans here! Can they help us? I want to shout out that we are being held hostage, that we are the captives of these men 'escorting' us. Perhaps these mining delegates can somehow save us. I look fleetingly at their faces and wonder if amongst these assembled businessman there might be a hero ready to spring forward.

But you know, I do nothing. I do not call out. For the insane reason that I do not wish to cause a scene. So strong is my conditioning that I feel unable to call for that help. How pathetic is that? But it is the truth. Do I just not want to be seen as a mad woman rambling? Would it make any difference if I cry out? Would any one of these delegates believe me let alone intervene? Would crying out make things worse for us, earn us a beating in some back room?

Who can know? But in my next life I won't be afraid to cause a riot. My close friends will attest to the fact that I am a tad confrontational by nature. Give me a cause to fight and I will wade in happily. But even the relatively short period of my captivity has eroded who I am. My inner bolshieness is much reduced.

So we walk through the foyer in silence. We are ushered into a lift. Two other people who attempt to get into the same lift are quickly discouraged with a shake of the head. They take one look at the thugs and rapidly move away.

Up we go. We are taken to the 12th floor. We are marched along the hallway. Brad goes into one room, two of the thugs remain outside, while Rupert and I are escorted into another room nearby. The door is closed behind us. I hear the key turn in the lock.

Rupert and I collapse on the bed. I had feared that we would be spending this night in prison. We are prisoners, but we are confined not to some terrible cell but to a perfectly nice hotel. In the midst of being unlucky, we are very lucky. It has been one of the most eventful days of my life, an emotional maelstrom. It's been bad, but it could have been so much worse.

Chapter Forty Five: Day 12

In the shower the next morning, Rupert tells me that he recognises the hotel that we have been taken to. You see, he has been to Teheran before. Twice.

It was when he worked as a merchant banker for Robert Fleming (the bank founded by the forebears of James Bond creator, Ian Fleming), that Rupert visited Iran. On his first trip, in 1999 he had a series of meetings with various ministries. He also went to several parties, including one where to his slight bemusement he was instructed by a charming elderly Iranian fixer in the etiquette of wine pouring. As an older teenager, this man had been to a finishing school in Switzerland where he had learned the exact level in a wine glass up to which white wine should be poured (one third full), and up to which level red wine should be poured (two thirds full). He was surprised and shocked that Rupert did not know this.

Rupert enjoyed his visit and also found it promising. On his return to London, he was enthusiastic about the prospect of doing business there. When he mentioned this to an Iranian contact, the man gave a rueful laugh. "You must go back again," he said. "I will arrange for you to see the other Iran."

There was something ominous in the man's tone, but Rupert took up his invitation and returned to Teheran. This time, he was taken to a series of meetings with a set of individuals who were radically different from those he had met on his first visit. These meetings were not with the Ministries, but with the men who ran the Bonyads, the state holding companies for the confiscated assets of the deposed Shah and his encircling elite.

These men were hard faced, hostile and not remotely interested in doing business with the West. To them, the West, and Rupert, were the enemy.

They were the Revolutionary Guard.

Rupert returned to London telling a very different story. There was no business to be done, and he had no desire to return to Teheran. To paraphrase *Invictus*, while we might just hope to be the masters of our soul, we are patently not always the captains of our ship...

These earlier visits to Teheran... They are problematic. If Rupert is asked has he been to Teheran before should he say yes and tell them about this or would it sound inherently suspicious? But if he says *no*, and it is somehow discovered that he *had* visited Teheran, then what would be the consequences of his lie?

We decide that it is highly unlikely that Iran's record-keeping will be of sufficient standard to betray his earlier visits. If we are asked, we shall both deny his ever having been here before. We can only pray it is the right decision. We emerge from the shower and dress quickly. I have taken to hiding Rupert's and my and Brad's passports on my person. My black Lycra dress is tight and so I keep the passports wedged against my stomach. I could conceal an awful lot of stuff under my chador. There is a brisk knock at the door. We look through the spy hole. A very smooth-looking individual in civilian clothes is standing outside. I think he can feel my scrutiny because he says, "Good morning. I'm from the Ministry of Information. I would like to talk to you. I'm going to come in."

Very sensitive of him. I could have been in a state of undress.

The door opens and in he comes. I glimpse Thug One glowering outside. This new man would appear to be in his late twenties, possibly early thirties. He looks as if his natural habitat would be a nightclub in a high-end city in a secular First World country. His chinos are well cut, his blue shirt is crisply ironed and fits snugly to his well-exercised body. He has wavy, collar-length hair. My mother would call him a lounge lizard. But he is much more dangerous than that. I can see the sharp intelligence flickering in his eyes.

He gestures us to the sofa, takes a seat opposite.

"So, tell me about Abu Musa. Tell me about *Sinbad* and your voyage to our island."

I do not waste time by arguing that it is not his island. If it were not so serious it would sound like a playground squabble. It's not yours, it's mine (well, the Emiratis' anyway). So we smoke and we tell him.

"You must tell me everything," he says. "I'm your friend. I'm here to get you out."

Rupert and I resist the temptation to glance at each other. I know what my husband is thinking. We both wish we could believe this poised individual with his American-accented perfect English. But we absolutely do not. He is as coiled, and as sinuous, and as poisonous as a beautiful snake.

We answer more of his questions and we smoke more cigarettes until we run out. Seeing that, he gets to his feet and raps sharply at the door. Thug Number One opens it.

"What brand would you like?" asks The Snake. "Marlborough Lights, please."

Five minutes later two packs arrive. With a quick glower at us, Thug One hands them over. We smoke some more, we talk some more. The Snake stands up.

"You must be hungry," he says. "What would you like for breakfast?"

We ate nothing the day before. We should be starving. Nerves have shredded our appetite but we need to eat. We've all lost weight. I'm now on the wrong side of skinny. Rupert, used to the rigours of hard exercise, has lost muscle. Brad's shorts are falling off him. We ask for toast and coffee. He leaves when our breakfast arrives, we suspect to talk to Brad.

Rupert and I turn on the television. There is Sky News. What luxury. If glamping is luxury camping then maybe we are being held hotelstage. There is animated debate on the subject of the day on the news reports. God is having another one of His cosmic jokes. The subject under discussion is the period of time for which detainees may be held by the UK authorities without being charged of a crime. Typically it has been up to two or three days. Now the security agencies are asking for an extension of up to twenty eight days' detention without charge so that they might investigate fully both the detainees and their computer hard drives and phones and their movements over the recent and less recent past. The investigation of terrorism suspects has of necessity taken a highly forensic turn and time is needed for these investigations. But sitting in Teheran, having been held for twelve days without being charged with any crime, I am rather appalled by the twenty eight day extension even though I'm normally rather hawk-like on law and order and counterterrorism issues.

I can only hope that the Iranians are not watching these debates. When I repeatedly tell them that it is wrong, illegal, iniquitous and unconscionable to keep holding us in this way, I am in danger of having lost the moral high ground.

There is a knock on the door and two new faces appear. So begins another seemingly endless process of interrogations by what we are guessing are multiple different ministries. We still do not know if we are being held under the auspices of the Revolutionary Guard or not.

When we are not being interrogated, Rupert and I turn on the television and we watch the ongoing debates about the twenty eight day rule. The other drama that plays out is the riots sweeping across major French cities. Are the Iranians watching this too, revelling in the seeming implosion of Western secular materialism?

Out comes Boggle again. We really are championship standard now.

Mr Smooth returns. We ask how Brad is. We're not allowed to see him. We ask that our Embassy representatives be allowed access to us. There is a polite shake of the head. We ask for our phone so that we might talk to our children. Again a shake of the head. I ask when we are going to be freed.

"Soon, *Inshallah*," says Mr Smooth. He seems to be our point man now.

"You need to give me your passports," he says. "I need to get them stamped with an Exit Visa."

"No," we say firmly. Rupert and I both have this belief that if we give away our passports we will never be freed. Neither of us can bring ourselves to trust this man despite his repeated requests that we do.

Chapter Forty Six: The Thug Attacks

Another evening and another night pass. Another day passes with endless interrogations. We are getting nowhere. I decide that I need to do something. We have not been allowed access to our phones so there is no way that I can smuggle out messages by text.

We are allowed to knock on the door and ask for room service via the Thugs. So this is what I do. I knock on the door, it is opened, not by Thug Number One, I see him some way down the corridor, but by a different thug. Nimbly, I duck through the open door and into the hallway. I sit down on the floor.

The Thugs all begin to yell at me in Farsi, gesticulating at the door. I shake my head. They scream some more. I refuse to move. Thug Number One marches up to me. I am very frightened that he is going to hit me. I'm relying on Islam to protect me. I can see his fists clenching. I know that he is longing to punch me. Somehow he manages to hold back and just screams at me, his face inches from mine. Another thug makes a call on his mobile. I look up and down the corridor hoping to see some Europeans, a friendly face that might report on the scene going on.

The British Embassy will have lost us. They will have no idea where we are being kept. If a witness can see a European woman albeit one covered in a chador and veil, gesticulating and arguing with a group of thugs perhaps the word will filter out. It is a risk I have to take.

The Thug continues screaming at me. I look away, refusing to move. I just shake my head and stay silent. After about five minutes Mr Smooth appears. For the first time, he appears rattled.

"What are you doing?" he asks. "Why are you doing this?"

"Because you are not letting us go. Because you are not letting us get in touch with our Embassy. Because you are not letting us talk to our children. Because nothing is happening! I'm not going to move until you let us talk to our Embassy."

"You cannot do it this way," he insists. "Be patient," he urges. "Please. You must go back inside now."

I stay where I am. "No," I say shaking my head. "I will not move until you let me call my Embassy."

Thug Number One is turning puce. He's marching up and down in front of me. I look away. There is a discussion in Farsi and then the door to our bedroom is thrown open by the Thug. The next thing I see is him dragging out my husband by his arm. He throws Rupert headfirst into the wall, then he starts to beat him up. Rupert does not defend himself. Any use of his skills would have been potentially dangerously revealing and would only have pulled in more of the thugs. But I'm not sure how long his self-control will last and I cannot bear to see him beaten up so I run into the room shouting and screaming at the Thug. It takes all my self-control not to grab him and try and pull him off my husband.

The door is slammed and locked behind us. "Are you all right?" I ask Rupert. He does not speak to me. He paces with the unspendable fury of a caged animal. I know I need to leave him alone so that he might recover his composure, dissipate this boiling rage that has nowhere to go. This powerlessness is like poison. And we have to just suck it up.

Have I done the right thing or have I made things worse for us?

Chapter Forty Seven: A Gift

There is a large window in our room. It is curtained with a veil of gauzy fabric. I push it aside and stand with my hands against the cold glass looking out across Teheran towards the distant mountains. I do this because my eyes at least have freedom. They can roam to those snow-capped peaks, as can my imagination. I also stand there in case there is anyone looking towards our hotel from one of the apartment or office blocks across the street. A member of our Embassy, perhaps. It is unlikely we will be spotted like this but it is an easy thing to do, to stand here with my forehead pressed against the cold glass, gazing out and waiting. It passes the time.

Several hours go by and Mr. Smooth reappears. He is carrying a cardboard box.

"I have been in touch with your Embassy," he says. "They have sent you some stuff." He puts down the box. There is a selection of paperbacks, well-thumbed treasures from somebody's library. There's also a sponge bag with a range of goodies – face creams and the like. The kindness of these gestures moves both Rupert and myself. "Now, you must give me your passports so that I can get the Exit Visas ready for you," continues Mr. Smooth.

I still do not trust this man. I shake my head. I keep the passports snug against my stomach.

Rupert has calmed down. We fall upon the new books. We eat dinner. We watch the riots on television. We wait for time to pass. Though we are exhausted we do not sleep well. Too many nightmares.

Chapter Forty Eight: Trust Me

Another day dawns. Mr. Smooth reappears. He comes and sits down opposite us on his customary chair while we sit on the sofa.

"Listen," he says, his eyes displaying a candour that I have not seen in them before. "You must trust me. You must give me your passports so that I can take them away and get Exit Visas. You will not go free otherwise."

Rupert and I look at each other. The gift from the Embassy could have been a fake but it felt real. That would suggest that this man has been in touch with them and that something positive might well be happening. We have to take the risk. We are getting desperate.

"Give me a moment," I say. I slip away into the bathroom and I remove our passports. I wave them in the air to cool them down. It feels too personal to hand them over when they still bear the warmth of my body.

Mr. Smooth takes them. "Thank you," he says getting to his feet. "Now I will go and I will get your visas."

Something inside me tells me to believe him. Is it blind hope, wishful thinking or are my instincts correct and will we really be freed?

Time will tell. We spend another interminable day waiting. I pick up a pen and paper and I write another poem.

How many?

How many cigarettes can you smoke in an hour?
How many seconds can you spend?
How much more will they try to rend
The heart of me apart?

How much hope can you raise in your soul
When they grab it and piss it away?
How much waiting can you endure,
Day after day after day?

Why do they try to break my spirit
By keeping me from all I hold dear?
By giving me words without meaning
And filling my heart with fear?

Chapter Forty Nine: Exit

Darkness is falling when Mr Smooth returns. He's holding up our passports and Brad's. He is smiling.

"I have your Exit Visas," he says. "You see, you were right to trust me. You are free. We leave for the airport now."

Adrenaline floods my body. Rupert and I look at each other, so many emotions flashing across our faces. Can this really finally be it? I don't dare hope so, but my body does. It hopes desperately. I can feel it yearning, trembling, burning with adrenaline.

We grab our things and Mr. Smooth leads us out into the corridor. Thug One is there glaring at us as usual. We collect Brad from his room. I'm so relieved to see him. He looks withdrawn, exhausted, but a faint fragile hope is lighting his eyes too.

We descend in the lift to the lobby. The international mining conference is over now. There are few people around. We walk out quickly to a waiting car. Thug Number One gets into the driver's seat. Mr. Smooth takes the seat beside him. Rupert, Brad and I squeeze into the back. The other thugs get into a car behind. We set off at breakneck speed.

The next sixty minutes are some of the most terrifying of my life. Is Thug Number One trying to murder us by causing a high-speed car crash? Kamikaze killing? Or is the man just a mindlessly stupid macho idiot who drives like this all the time?

I honestly do not know how we avoid a crash but somehow, miraculously, we arrive at the airport with the car intact and our nerves shredded.

There is a plane waiting. It has been held for us. We are whisked through the airport. Mr. Smooth leads the way while the band of Thugs walk alongside and behind us as we hurry to the departure gate. Tickets are waiting for us at the desk. The thugs remain standing, watching us. Thug Number One does not take his eyes off us until we have passed through the final check and walked through the security doors. We hurry down out onto the tarmac.

Mr. Smooth leads us towards the waiting plane. "This will take you to Qatar," he says. "From there you will get another flight that your Embassy has booked to take you to Dubai."

Have we really made it? We three look at each other, then we turn to him. "Thank you," we say. He nods, and he walks away.

Before we can start to walk up the steps onto the plane we see a figure approaching. Thug Number One. Has he come to stop us? Please God no. Hearts racing, we rush up the steps. We hold out our tickets. A flight steward checks them and ushers us on board. We take our seats. The doors close. Seconds pass. Minutes pass. We can hardly breathe. We sit in silence. And then very slowly our plane begins to reverse away from the gate.

As it turns, I see standing on the tarmac his features cast daemonic orange by the security lights, Thug Number One. Then the plane taxis towards the runway and I can see him no more. The plane stops. We hear the engines rev and then it begins its long lumbering acceleration down the runway. As its wheels leave the tarmac, I finally begin to believe we are free.

Chapter Fifty: To Freedom

The plane gains height. The lights of Teheran fade. We fly across the snow-capped mountains of the Elburz. I feel a lightness as if I too am flying.

Rupert and I sit for a while in silence, very much together, periodically squeezing each other's hands, but each of us is processing. There is so much to sift through and rationalise. Too much. So many emotions are bubbling round my body but the one I hone in on is wild joy.

Sparkling wine is served. Across the aisle from us, by the window, sits Brad. Some European stranger sits between us and him. He watches as we raise our glasses.

"To freedom!" we say, and we start to laugh, wonderful not quite hysterical, joyous laughter. We drain our glasses. The man is looking bemused, a question in his eyes.

"We are toasting our freedom," we say. "We've been held hostage by the Iranians. And we have been let go."

He nods, he says nothing. Perhaps he doesn't know what to say. Or perhaps he just doesn't believe us.

In the years to come, when I look back on these two weeks, sometimes I'm not even sure I believe it happened myself.

Chapter Fifty One: Home

We transit via Qatar. Now that home is within my reach I can hardly contain my impatience.

We land in Dubai airport. I've always been nervous in airports. Freudians say they represent a transition which can be seen as death. I wouldn't go that far, but I've had a number of unpleasant experiences in various airports around the world, from being shaken down in Bogota by corrupt airline officials who claimed my ticket was 'wrong,' but could be corrected for four hundred dollars, to US Immigration who said the visa I was trying to enter with was no longer valid despite the date saying it was, sorted out by a call to my Embassy, to Stalinist officials in pre-fall of the Berlin Wall Bulgaria who for a few dire hours tried to stop me transiting through their country, until I pointed out that delightful as their country no doubt was, I was very keen to get to Egypt and perhaps they might just allow me to lighten my load by taking my duty free perfume and then board my plane.

And then of course I can add my Iranian airport experiences to the list...

So I get antsy in airports. There is too much that can go wrong. As we bypass the baggage collection I'm worrying that we might have a problem at Immigration. We have no exit stamp from when we left Dubai. Officials hate irregularities and any explanation we come up with would be a tad complicated... I wonder whether we will be met by anyone who might smooth our way.

It is weird. We pass through Immigration with a smile and a wave and a friendly *Assalam Aleikum*, to be met on the other side by a representative of the British Embassy. It is now very late at night, or rather very early in the morning. The man looks tired.

"Rupert and Linda Wise, Brad Shulton," he says, less of a question than a statement.

We nod, reach out, shake his hand.

"Welcome home," he says.

We thank him. We've been dreading some kind of debrief, any delay that keeps us from our children, but there is none. We exchange the minimum of small talk, then the man walks away.

We three stand in the shockingly bright lights of the airport, blinking. Free…

For two weeks, every second of our time belonged to our captors. Our self-determination was pretty much non-existent. Now it is absolute.

We walk out into the hot Dubai night. The familiar mix of petrol fumes, dust and sweat hits me. We head for the taxis. I keep looking around, as if Thug Number One might materialise, or else have arranged for some of his Dubai-based henchmen to intercept us. Despite the hour, the airport is still busy, but I can't see any Thug Figures, just the normal ebb and flow of Emiratis in their Thobes and Pakistanis and Afghanis in their shalwar kameezes. Everyone looks relaxed, normal. There is none of the hunter's visceral hunger on any of these faces.

We bid goodbye to Brad. "Keep in touch," we say.

He nods. 'Will do.' We hug each other, then he ducks into a taxi and disappears.

The next taxi in the queue pulls up. I peer through the glass at the driver. The Iranians have exported their paranoia to me… But the man seems innocuous: courteous, tired, phlegmatic at the end of a long shift. We hop in, sink back against the crackling plastic seats. The taxi lurches forward into the night, out onto the freeway.

Every familiar landmark is a joy to me: Dubai Creek with the lights of the pleasure boats shimmering on the dark water; the twin spires of Emirates Towers shining out across Sheikh Zayed Road; the now dark side streets housing the Jumeirah Primary School, Hugh and Tom's school. And then our house, all lights off, sleeping in the darkness.

The taxi drops us off on Al Manara Street. We glance around. There is no visible tail. The road is deserted. We let ourselves in. I look at Rupert. Neither of us can quite believe we are here. We lock the door behind us and creep through the silent house.

We go first to the shared bedroom of our boys, Hugh and Tom. We gaze down at their sleeping bodies. I feel a surge of such happiness and pain it threatens to overwhelm me. I reach down, stroke their hair. We wake them gently, whispering into their ears. "It's Mummy and Daddy. We're back. We're home." They surface from deep sleep, they blink at us in the darkness. We hold them, moving from one boy to the other, hugging them tight, kissing their faces. "Now go back to sleep," we say. "We'll talk in the morning. Everything's fine." And with that great capacity that children have, they fall asleep again.

We tuck them in and tiptoe out, to our daughter's room. She is lying on her back in her cot bed. Rupert stands motionless, breathing in the sight of her. He reaches down, strokes her cheek and then he turns to leave.

I stand there, looking down at her. I had thought, I had feared on several occasions that I would never see my children's faces again, that they were lost to me and I was lost to them forever. To be back here with them, to be reunited with them, to be able to reach out and touch them, to have my husband, their father home with us, is everything to me. My heart cannot contain the joy and the pain. I fall to my knees and I weep silently.

Epilogue One

We awoke early the next morning to find ourselves in the middle of something of a media storm. Our phone rang continuously (the canny media had somehow got our number). Back in the UK, my brother, Roy's, work phone's incessant ringing disturbed the peace and bemused his colleagues at Exeter University (he had through sheer coincidence taken the day off).

We declined all interview requests save one: As our friend Frank Gardner of the BBC had been so helpful behind the scenes in securing our release, we were more than happy to speak to him and to the local representatives of the BBC in Dubai. I did not want to give the interview in front of our children, so Rupert and I went outside where we would not be overheard.

It felt surreal to be sitting in our garden in sunshine under an open sky talking about our experiences seemingly in another world. In another life almost. Even back then, I had begun the distancing act that made it feel as if I were talking about something that happened to somebody else, not to me.

Rupert did a number of additional interviews on BBC Radio. It seems that a surprisingly high number of our friends have radios in their bathrooms, some even in their showers, for they told us later how as they were going about their morning ablutions they yelled in alarm when they heard Rupert's voice emerging from the radio describing the events of the preceding weeks. Of course, almost none of our friends knew about what had happened to us so at least this way the first thing they heard was the good news that we had been released and we were home safe. I suppose it was one way of updating them. Rather more immediate than a round robin email.

As well as television and radio interest there was also very considerable print media attention. We were offered large sums of money to give our first-hand accounts, which we declined. But I knew that our story would be told and I wanted to take some control over how it would be presented, so I decided to tell it in my own words. I wrote an article for the *Daily Telegraph* newspaper. It appeared on the front page the next day. After I had given the interview to the BBC and written the article for the *Daily Telegraph* I withdrew from the media world and publically, I neither said nor wrote any more on the subject. Our kidnapping and release was reported widely in the international media. It also rather worryingly but predictably made the press in Iran. Payvand's *Iran News* quoted British Foreign Secretary Jack Straw (who had been interviewed by BBC Radio Four's flagship current affairs *Today Programme*) During that interview, Straw had said, "I'm very glad that the Wises have been released safely and without any charge by the Iranians. It took a good deal of work behind the scenes to achieve this result and I'm just relieved that we have got there." Straw went on to say that the incident had been "distressing for the Wises and for their family." He spelt out that military action against Iran was "inconceivable."

Rupert, having declined to be interviewed by any of the newsprint media, paid the price in that he could not control in any way how they presented him. An article appeared describing him in a rather sensationalist headline as *"The banker with a CV out of a spy novel."* Amusing with hindsight though not at the time.

But it was done. Our story had been told. The beginning and the end. It could now be forgotten. We could move on. Get back to normal life…

Epilogue Two

The next weeks were a bit of a blur. My daughter was ill. My nanny told me that she was a bit poorly, but when I took her to the doctor first thing the next morning it transpired that Lara had pneumonia. She had also developed separation anxiety and for the next year she could not be parted from me. Everywhere I went, Lara went. The boys handled it better, but who knows what goes on deep in the psyche. Hugh developed a passion for architecture, endlessly describing his ideal house which was basically an impregnable fort surrounded by armed guards. Doesn't take a psychiatrist to work out what was going on in his mind. Tom is more happy-go-lucky, he just seemed to accept that sometimes bad stuff happens and then you simply move on. A valuable life lesson, but perhaps one that at five years old is a bit too early to have to learn.

Mercifully, if surprisingly, neither Rupert nor I was called in to our Embassy, nor were we visited, for any kind of debrief. We had both dreaded having to go over those events again. We just wanted to put it all behind us, almost to pretend it had never happened. Denial can be a useful coping mechanism.

A couple of days after our release, Rupert returned to his office and threw himself back into his work. I didn't want to work. I didn't want to carry on with my writing at that stage and besides I needed to be with my children all the time. As much for my sake as for theirs. Happily, within a couple of weeks Lara had recovered from her pneumonia. She was fine, as long as she could see me.

I found it hard to shake my paranoia. When I was driving I constantly watched the rear view mirror, checking for tails. I couldn't quite believe that the Iranians had relinquished us. I found myself plunging into a depression. I had always written about the tightrope between a good, secure and happy life on one side and the maelstrom of misadventure on the other. I was too aware of the proximity of disaster and felt an unaccustomed vulnerability. I felt like a shadow; thin, weak and vulnerable. I needed to build myself up in every sense.

I carried on smoking for a while, which wasn't ideal, but it did give rise to one amusing incident. Rarely in life do we get the opportunity to come up with the perfect one-liner. This was one of those wonderful times…

I went to the beach at the Jumeirah Beach Club with my friend Sarah Turner (she who had held the fort so wonderfully at home) and her three children. We got there early, so we lined up six sun loungers in prime position overlooking the sea (the two youngest would share with Mummy). In a little while we would perch on the loungers to have a delicious lunch. Sheer luxury! In the meantime, we messed about, running in and out of the sea, swimming, building sand castles, periodically retreating to the shade of the sun loungers with their overhead umbrellas. After a while, Sarah's youngest became overtired and she took her home to put her to bed while I stayed on the beach building more sand castles with her other two children and my three. The beach filled up around us as more people arrived and claimed the best spots.

Sometime later, up sauntered a groovy young couple with their take-out Starbucks cups and a beach attendant in tow, in search of prime beachfront. They eyed the six sun loungers stretched out behind me with a covetous air. "What about taking two of those?" the man asked the beach attendant, gesturing to my rank of sun loungers. At that point Sarah's eldest child Jack, turned to me as I casually smoked my cigarette and remarked, "Linda, I didn't know you smoked. When did you start smoking?"

I turned to him and I said loudly enough for my voice to carry, "When I was in prison, Jack."

The Starbucks couple rapidly decided that my sun loungers were no longer quite so attractive. Giggling to myself I watched them walk off.

There's always a silver lining.

I explained to my children why I smoked at that time (I never smoked in the house, always outside, some distance from them). I told them that while smoking was bad for me, it had comforted me when I was under fairly extreme pressure. I reassured them that I intended to give it up imminently, that I was getting stronger every day and soon would not want or need that prop. I thought it better to reveal human frailty and weakness rather than papering it over and pretending I was invulnerable. I smoked my last cigarette before we got on the plane for the long flight to Auckland for our Christmas holiday.

New Zealand was beautiful and balmy. The food and wine were delicious. We had three weeks of family time exploring that gorgeous country, bathing in thermal lakes, hiking ancient forests, and celebrating Christmas.

On the morning of the 25th, we went to a beautiful old wooden church filled with farmers and their children. The service was taken by a woman minister who gave us a wonderfully warm welcome. During prayers, I found myself crying silent tears of gratitude. Thanking God, thanking the fates, thanking all those who helped secure our release and those who held the fort for us during our captivity.

After church we returned to our lodge, opened our presents and sat down to a delicious feast in a beautiful red room overlooking the distant whitecaps of Palliser Bay.

I felt that I had regained myself. And my life.

The five of us were together. We were free.

And that was everything.

Postscript One

We never saw Brad again. I tried to get in contact with him but he seemed to have vanished. His old Dubai phone number was discontinued. When I attempted to track him down via Duboats, I was told that he had spent three days in a hotel in Dubai, then resigned. Apparently, he then flew to Malaysia, a place he spoke of often and longingly when we were in captivity. I don't know if it is apocryphal or true, but Duboats told me that shortly after arriving there, Brad married a bar girl. Either way, I wish him happiness in his freedom.

Postscript Two

One of the questions we are often asked, is *did we get our boat back?* And the answer to this is yes, after some considerable time and after another Tom Clancy-esque episode, we did get our boat back. Or perhaps I should say our boat was got back for us.

In 2006, our first approach was to our insurance company. We never thought we would get back our boat, so this was the logical step. We had a policy, it seemed watertight (forgive me). Reimbursement should be a straightforward process. In theory.

So we went along for a meeting. We explained how we had been kidnapped at sea and our boat had been taken by the Iranians. A pure case of theft you might think.

But no, living up to the worst preconceptions of their genre, the insurance company started a process of prolonged wriggling which began as follows:

"Ah, Abu Musa, well, terribly sorry, but that's outside the territory of the United Arab Emirates. *Not covered!*"

"Oh really," we replied. "Perhaps you would like to tell Sheikh Mohammed bin Zayed Al Nahayan, the United Arab Emirates Foreign Minister, that you do not consider Abu Musa to be Emirati territory. He might be a tad surprised as he has made a series of speeches at the United Nations setting out that Abu Musa is the sovereign territory of the United Arab Emirates and is being occupied illegally by Iran."

There followed rapid backtracking. The UAE is a strictly hierarchical country and the insurance company realised that this was a supremely foolish tack for them to take.

The next attempt to refuse to pay went as follows. "Ah, Iran, you say.

Your boat was taken by the Iranian state. That is an Act of State! That is force majeure! That is a terrorist act! Very sorry but no. Not covered!"

After months of this, it became evident this was a battle we were not going to win. So we gave up and refocused our energies on getting the boat back.

It was now 2007. Rupert was introduced to an Iranian lawyer based in Dubai. A long process of discussions ensued. In August of 2007, they heated up. First of all, we were told that we had to pay 'mooring fees'. It was calculated that many months of mooring fees care of the Iranian government would amount to the sum of $25,000.

However unpalatable this thinly disguised bribe might have been, economically it made sense to pay it in order to get our boat back. Let's be clear here: we did not intend to sail on *Sinbad* ever again. That dream had long since been shattered. We just wanted to get her back, spruce her up and sell her to someone who could enjoy her.

Rupert was told that he needed to pay the $25,000 into the Dubai branch of the Dubai Islamic bank. So he rang up his bank in the UK and began the process of making the transfer.

"What is the purpose of these funds?" asked the person at his bank.

"You do not need to know the purpose of the funds," replied Rupert. "All you need to know is the source of funds. That is me and you have done exhaustive KYC (Know Your Client) due diligence on me." Technically, Rupert was correct but nobody seemed to have told the person on the other end of the line that. They persisted for a good few minutes with a level of obstinacy familiar to anybody who has ever attempted to extract a service from their bank.

"I must know the purpose of the funds," this person continued to demand.

Finally, Rupert cracked. "You really want to know?"

"I really want to know."

"Right, well here it is. This $25,000 is to pay a bribe to the Iranian government to release our boat. In 2005, we were taken hostage by the Iranian authorities and although we were released, our boat was not. In order to secure the return of our boat we have to pay a bribe of $25,000. That is the purpose of the money. Does that answer your question?"

There was a lengthy silence at the other end of the line, followed by an:

"Oh, I see. Right then…"

So the money was transferred into the account at Dubai Islamic bank.

Then the handover had to be arranged.

"Would you like to sail out into international waters and take possession of your yacht at midnight in four days' time, at a location fifteen nautical miles due south of Abu Musa?" The Iranian lawyer asked us.

"Er, I think that would be a definite No," we answered. There was no amount of money in the world that would induce either of us to do that.

"OK. You don't want to miss your window, you know."

"What window?"

"The moon."

"What about the moon?"

"In four days' time it will be a moonless night."

Well that's reassuring. "So let's get this straight, we are meant to set sail on a moonless night and rendezvous somewhere far offshore with the Iranians at midnight?"

"Yes exactly!"

"We think perhaps we'd rather not."

So, impasse. Until an action man who was willing to do just that for a fee came along. A former Royal Navy man, an adept sailor, and an adrenaline junkie, was up for it. We told him of the risks. He was nonchalant. He and a fellow Royal Navy friend of his set sail.

I did not sleep the night that they went out to reclaim our boat. They rang when they were back in Dubai in the morning, safe and sound, to my intense relief.

We found out later why the boat was handed over in such a clandestine way. It was a familiar story of Iranians being terrified of other Iranians. *Sinbad* was in the possession of the Iranian Navy, the mainstream Iranian Navy. They wished to hand the boat over thereby claiming the 'mooring fees' without the knowledge of the naval part of the Revolutionary Guard who regularly patrolled those waters. Again, the spectre of the Revolutionary Guard loomed large.

It made me think of all the different Irans: the Revolutionary Guard themselves with all the sinister forces at their command; the Security Services such as VEVAK who turn civilian neighbours into enemies, denouncing any perceived heresies or criticism of the regime; the screamingly censorious Ayatollahs berating their enraptured or terrified followers; the ordinary Iranians who I realise with some poignancy are hostages to their totalitarian and brutal regime. For them there is no escape…

Rupert set off that same morning to take a look at our boat. I did not wish to see her. There were too many bad memories and no good ones to balance them.

Rupert returned home a few hours later and said: "She's in pretty good nick, actually. And get this! We have now acquired ten fishing rods of various descriptions and about a dozen lifejackets ranging from adult right down to toddler size."

I burst out laughing. So the Iranians in Bandar Abbas had been using *Sinbad* as a pleasure boat. I hoped it was Reza and Ali who had gone out with their families and had some fun aboard her. It was good that someone did. Rupert also gave me a stripy orange towelling top that I had left aboard *Sinbad*. I still have it. I pull it on when I've been swimming in the sea and I need a bit of instant warmth. My souvenir, my reminder if ever I need it, of the lessons I have learned…

We sold *Sinbad*. I was happy to bid her and the dreams that went with her, goodbye. I had no desire to sail again. Show me a sea and I will swim in it. Despite my Viking heritage, I will leave the sailing to others.

When God gives you a cosmic message of the magnitude that He sent us during those two weeks in Iran, you'd best listen.

Afterword, February 2014

It is now nearly ten years since we were kidnapped. I realise that we were immensely lucky that we were held for only two weeks. The thing about those two weeks was at no point during that time were we aware that it was to be only two weeks. Had we known that, it would have been much easier to manage our time but we did not know and we had good reason to think that we might be held for many years.

We weren't and for that I will be forever grateful. At about the same time as we were kidnapped, two other sailors, a French game boat captain and his German client were also kidnapped whilst sailing in the Persian Gulf. They were held for eighteen months in Evin Prison in Teheran.

I realise our period of confinement is miniscule compared to many of the long-term hostages and that our suffering was negligible compared to theirs. I do not write this book with any sense of a hierarchy of suffering.

I write it because it is my story and because I have always used my writing as a way of making sense of the world around me.

I had buried it all deep in my subconscious. Whenever the faces of newly-taken hostages appeared on my TV screen, I felt a profound sympathy. What I did not allow myself to feel, was empathy. Although I knew that, yes, I had been kidnapped, I always felt as if it had happened to somebody else. If I were put in a situation where I had to answer people who asked me directly about my experiences, I would baldly relay the facts in highly abbreviated form as if it were someone else's tale. This was not a story about me and my husband. Only of course, it was. When a few months ago I sat down at home to watch Ben Affleck's brilliant *Argo* with Rupert and our children, my heart pounded and I felt hardly able to breathe. I thought that perhaps it was time for a form of catharsis. It has not been an easy story to write. I wept while writing chunks of it. Emotions that I had long since buried were released. I glimpsed the edges of that almost overwhelming pain and despair that I had felt all those years ago. But I'm glad that I have written it for it reminded me of the lessons that I have learned. Chief amongst those are a sense of perspective and gratitude.

There are few problems that cannot be rendered insignificant when I stack them alongside our experiences in those two weeks, when I compare them to a situation where I might never have seen my children again, where I might have lost my life and my husband his.

The gratitude I had first felt upon my release has mellowed into a daily appreciation of all that I have, as opposed to a haunted awareness of all that I so nearly lost.

Getting kidnapped was a fairly extreme way to go about expanding my consciousness and gaining insight, but I am grateful for the lessons learned. Perhaps the most powerful is that all I need to feel a surge of happiness and calm is to walk into my children's bedrooms and watch them sleeping, or to look across the room at them, or even better, to reach out and be able to touch all three of them with my husband by my side.

Appendices

- Appendix One: Rupert's article for his old school, Marlborough College

- Appendix Two: Roger Cooper's kidnap and imprisonment

APPENDIX ONE

Rupert's article for his old school, Marlborough College.

A MISADVENTURE IN THE ARABIAN GULF

It was when the Iranian Navy boats slammed into both sides of our yacht and the armed marines came swarming aboard yelling at us to stand still that I realised I might have made a slight error of judgement.

I had bought the yacht, a 38-foot Catamaran, three days before and this was supposed to have been an idyllic overnight cruise in the Arabian Gulf to test the boat and its systems. The error of judgment had come in trying to pick an anchorage away from the jet skis, light pollution, and fisherman's vessels of Dubai.

Fifty miles due North of Dubai lay the Island of Abu Musa, isolated, clearly on 'our' side of the Gulf and seemingly perfect for our purposes. I duly instructed our skipper to find out everything he could about it, and then blithely headed out on a short business trip.

The great day dawned, the last Friday of Ramadan towards the end of October 2005, and the good ship *Sinbad* duly set sail with my wife, Linda, and me and an Australian skipper.

Seven hours later, at 3:45 pm, with the yacht behaving perfectly, we motored slowly into a large bay on the Western shore of Abu Musa Island looking for a suitable place to anchor for the night. The sleepy, humid torpor of the Ramadan afternoon was duly shattered by seemingly the entire Iranian Naval base overcompensating for having been so fast asleep as to allow a strange vessel to penetrate twelve miles into their territorial waters and nearly drop anchor on the edge of their jealously guarded port. After a tricky few hours of being continually shouted at in Farsi and, at one stage, of being towed out to sea and being lined up and having guns cocked and pointed at us, a relative form of sanity seemed to prevail and *Sinbad* was tied up to the quay of the Naval base and we were put under guard for the night on board the yacht. Not quite the overnight experience we had hoped for on the yacht's inaugural voyage!

Our first day in captivity dawned and amidst all the inevitable recriminations as to whose fault this was (mine I'm afraid!). I remembered one of my survival instructors (from a course I attended some 25 years ago) saying that what really kills a lot of people in survival situations is plummeting morale and a feeling of overwhelming stupidity that they had allowed themselves to get into such a dire situation in the first place. I felt like a prime candidate!

Morale was partially restored by card games, a very competitive word game called 'Boggle' (we were due to become experts at this over the next two weeks of our captivity) and a smooth interrogator from Iranian Naval Intelligence, who kept promising imminent release without ever actually delivering (I was put in mind of a debate at Marlborough on the proposition that *"If ignorance is bliss, 'tis folly to be wise."* Ignorance, or at least false hope, proved to be quite sustaining for a while!).

The next stage in the saga arrived when we were ordered to be flown to the coastal Iranian city of Bandar Abbas, just inside the Straits of Hormuz at the mouth of the Arabian Gulf. There then followed a short journey which consisted of being bundled into a Soviet era propeller-driven plane by bearded guards with guns, a short flight, being hustled into a mini-van with blackout curtains on the windows and finally arriving at a heavily guarded and curtained house on the Iranian Naval base in Bandar Abbas.

The following eleven days became a blur of different interrogation teams from various ministries, the navy and the judiciary all with their video cameras and recording equipment. During this period I made the mistake of letting slip some Arabic (I was born in British-administered South Yemen and consider Arabic my second language) in the naïve belief that a few Islamic greetings would establish common ground and make our captors more friendly. Big mistake! Huge! It made them doubly suspicious of us.

In the meantime, whilst I was putting into play my dimly remembered resistance to interrogation techniques (another course yet again many, many years ago!) to little or no effect, my wife was performing a tour de force. With a woman's (and mother's) unerring instincts she had spotted our captor's weak spots namely their intense discomfort as Muslim men in holding an innocent (they worked this out in the first 24 hours) Woman, Wife and Mother as a potential pawn in the great game. Using the "Thatcher technique" of choosing one or two big ideas ("You're all Fathers, how can you do this to a Mother?" and "You're all Husbands, how can you do this to a Wife?") and sticking to them, Linda handbagged them relentlessly day and night never once letting up and throwing in tears every now and then for good measure. The Foreign Office later told us that this is what had finally cracked the Iranians. On my own – I and the Australian Skipper, in their opinion, would probably still be there!

Another key ingredient was being able to get a message out to Frank Gardner (O.M., friend, senior BBC correspondent and survivor of 6 bullets fired into him by Al Qaeda in Riyadh) under the noses of 3 interrogators standing over us whilst I ostensibly telephoned our children in Dubai (another concession, ground out of our captors by Linda!). That and Linda's ability to text whilst appearing to have difficulty getting through to Dubai, meant that the Foreign Office knew within 5 days of our capture where we were and had a very incentivised Foreign Minister driving them on (Jack Straw having been informed by Frank of our captivity in the first place knew that the BBC would, after the event, have perfect 20/20 hindsight into his conduct).

The penultimate scene of our captivity comprised of our release after 11 days into the custody of the First Secretary of the British Embassy, who had flown down to Bandar Abbas, our re-arrest at Bandar Abbas airport just as we were about to board a flight out to Dubai (I suppose that it is character building at least once in one's life to know utter despair, but it didn't seem particularly wonderful at the time!), being flown under guard to Tehran, being thrown around in a blacked out minivan conducting evasive driving from the Airport whilst being guarded by two unsmiling armed policemen (we were manhandled into a second vehicle after 5 minutes – presumably to throw off any would-be James Bond following us from the British Ambassador's abortive reception committee at the airport) and arriving at our final destination for the night. We had successfully been made to disappear a second time!

The final scene consisted of yet another bit of the Iranian bureaucracy trying to decide whether to let us go or to charge us with something /anything. However, yet again Linda was the grit in the machine – the announcement "We've caught the British Spy/Bomber/ Whatever…and his WIFE" didn't quite work as a headline to whip the masses up into a fever of anti-western outrage. Thus it was that after another 3 days wondering whether this was going to be the pattern for the next 5 - 10 years of our lives, it was suddenly announced that we were free to go!

Perhaps the most frightening comment in retrospect was that of the British Embassy official taking charge of us at our release. "Can you tell me who exactly it is you think has been holding you?"

"Those people," says I, pointing to our 8 or so captors.

"Yes, but who are they and which organisation do they represent? We have no real idea!" By some miracle we had been permitted to escape, twice, from a Kafka-esque maze of competing Iranian government organisations all of whom had at some point over the last two weeks sized us up for whatever scintilla of political advantage we might offer them and had rejected us. Statistically and with hindsight this remains a highly unlikely outcome.

As the plane's wheels left the tarmac of Imam Khomeini International Airport and the celebratory champagne slid down, I tried to think positively and to come up with the (any!) improving lessons to be learnt from this debacle and could only come up with (a) stick close to your Wife - her instincts for the emotional jugular are far more developed than any mere man's, (b) this was a very elaborate way of telling us that we are not meant to have toys (still haven't got the yacht back!) and (c) everyone should have, and be aware of having, an inner core of real friends to whom one can turn when one gets into very serious trouble (and if one of them happens to be an Old Marlburian then so much the better!).

APPENDIX TWO

Roger Cooper's kidnap and imprisonment

In 1987, Roger Cooper was tried and convicted as a British spy. He was sentenced to "death plus ten years". He served his sentence in Evin Prison in Teheran, one of the most feared prisons in the world, where hundreds died before the Ayatollah's revolution and tens of thousands during and after it.

Cooper spent five years undergoing intensive interrogation and suffering frequent periods of solitary confinement. Following a rapprochement between Britain and Iran, he was released in April 1991.

Roger's book, *Death Plus Ten Years*, is still in print and is available on Amazon.

Acknowledgements

There are three sets of people whom I would like to thank profoundly.

The first is those people who set us free and those who looked after things at home during our captivity.

Many people worked behind the scenes to secure our release after they were first notified by Rupert's Office Manager, Robert Lawson, whose quick-thinking and ability to spot and decipher a code were crucial. Our friends, Sarah and Malcolm Turner, were the first to sound the alarm, and were wonderful at helping to look after and distract our children during those awful two weeks, including throwing a birthday party for Tom, who turned five in our absence.

There were many people at the Foreign Office whose names I was never given, or am unable to use, who worked on our release. I know that the Foreign Secretary, Jack Straw, played an active part. There were many others who worked tirelessly, among other things, ringing my mother and Rupert's mother on a daily basis to keep them informed and updated.

The Foreign Office officials in Iran, including the wonderful Iranian woman whom I have called Nasrin, played an essential role. In particular, I will never forget Nasrin's kindness. I would also like to thank those of our captors, and they will know who they are, who treated us kindly and gently and whose belief in our innocence helped secure our release. We were held hostage for two weeks but these people are in many ways held hostage for life by their own regime.

And own our unofficial team of friends, to whom we managed to get word of our captivity, played a crucial role: Frank Gardner, OBE who liaised closely with the Foreign Office and also ensured, critically, that there was a media blackout of our kidnap during the period of our detention; General

Sir Peter de la Billière; Sir Graham Boyce; and Adam Kelliher who was on the verge of chartering a plane to fly us out of Iran when we were released.

Then I would like to thank all those people who helped make this book a reality.

The first is my friend, the dean of investigative journalism, Ed Epstein. When I met up with him last year in New York and mentioned in passing my kidnap and captivity, he looked at me in astonishment and said: *'My Gad Linda, you have to write this story!'* So I did… I had studiously avoided thinking about it in the nine years since it happened but now with this book in front of me and I am delighted that I took Ed's advice.

Then there is my wonderful publisher, Vigliano Books. The brilliant and creative David Vigliano is always supportive and was super-enthusiastic about the project. Thomas Flannery Jr has put in an enormous amount of work on this book, from conjuring the beautiful map and cover design to wrestling with my photographs and my word document to being endlessly enthusiastic and supportive. It can get lonely up here in my writing tower and the support of these people, these friends, is essential.

I would also like to thank Marija Vilotijevic and Anthony Foley for the original cover and map respectively. Stunning designs and super creative.

Last of all I would like to thank my family.

First of all, my husband again, for his strength and his love and his wisdom during our captivity and in our life. And I would like to thank my children. Our ordeal was their ordeal too. They are now remarkably matter-of- fact and refer to all this as 'Mummy and Daddy's hostage thing.' They'll tell me this is cheesy but I don't care. They bring me so much joy. A few tears yes, but massive joy and meaning and purpose. I thank them for being them.

Here's to freedom!

— Linda, June, 2014

About the Author

Born in Scotland and raised in South Wales, Linda inhaled books as child and dreamed of becoming a writer. But she was the daughter of an economist and a homemaker and raised to be practical. So she went into investment banking instead. One day, to her horror, she figured out a way to commit the perfect financial crime.

Instead of doing it, she quit her job and wrote about it. *Nest of Vipers* went on to be published in over 30 territories, optioned multiple times and has sold over three million copies.

Linda has gone on to publish 11 more books, 6 for adults and 5 for children, which collectively have sold millions of copies and won various awards.

She has lived in Peru and the Middle East with her husband and 3 children. In 2005, in what could have been ripped from the pages of her own books she and her husband were kidnapped, interrogated and held prisoner in Iran. She went on to write about this experience and what she learned from it in her first work of non-fiction, *Kidnapped*.

Linda also writes for *The Times*, *Sunday Times*, *Daily Telegraph*, *Independent* and the *Guardian* newspapers and the National Theatre. She is a winner of the Philip Geddes Prize for journalism. In 2019, Linda became the Inaugural Writer in Residence at St Edmund Hall, University of Oxford.

She lives near the sea in Suffolk with her family and two Rhodesian Ridgebacks.

Printed in Great Britain
by Amazon

37253152R00088